IN THE TRACKS OF MORTALITY: THE LIFE AND TIMES OF ROBERT PATERSON, STONECUTTER, 1716-1801

IAIN WILSON

First published 2016 by Alba Printers Ltd
1 St Michael Street, Dumfries, DG1 2QD

Copyright © 2016 by Iain Wilson
Old Post Cottage, Keir Mill, Thornhill,
Dumfries & Galloway DG3 4DE

The right of Iain Wilson to be identified as the author of this work has been asserted by him in accordance with the Copyright, Design and Patents Act 1988.

British Library Cataloguing in Publication Data.
A catalogue record for this book is available from the British Library.

ISBN 978-0-9554737-3-9

Book and cover design by Alba Printers Ltd, Dumfries

To Jill
For her patience

CONTENTS

INTRODUCTION

This book explores the life and times of a stonemason who lived and worked in Scotland during the greater part of the eighteenth century and until the first year of the nineteenth century. Before his death he was already well known in Dumfriesshire, Galloway and Ayrshire, in the south-west of the country, and possibly in other parts of Scotland as well. He travelled regularly between towns and villages in the region where he devoted his energies to carving and erecting, engraving and cleaning the gravestones of the Covenanters, Protestant fundamentalists of the seventeenth century, many of whom were killed in running battles with, or as fugitives from, the forces of the state.

The story is interesting enough in its own right but probably would not have survived in any detail into the present day had 'Old Mortality', as he was nicknamed, not acquired greater fame several years after his death when he featured in a novel of the same title by Sir Walter Scott. The character of the archaic, rather grumpy old man, as Scott portrayed him, caught the popular imagination enough to encourage the novelist to delve more deeply into his real life story for the introduction to a later edition, leaving to posterity a formal record of a man whom history might otherwise have neglected. The literary connection, how it came about and its legacy form a central theme of this book.

Despite this, the facts available to us about Old Mortality, or Robert Paterson to give him his real name, are desperately few and difficult to add to after all these years. There was only one firsthand account of his life, and that relatively concise, plus two or three contemporary descriptions. Another, secondary account, was provided to Scott by the customs officer and antiquarian Joseph Train and forms the basis for the popular story which has come down to us today. It is based on the original account but embellishes and contradicts it in several respects. During the rest of the nineteenth century and the early years of the twentieth a number of other historians wrote about Paterson adding the results of new research or their own interpretations of his lifestyle to the mix but little other information to add context to or to bring his tale to life.

Unearthing the real story of Paterson's life is a second theme of the chapters that follow. To fill the gaps it was necessary, not just to look at old records and manuscripts which might hold new clues to what Paterson did and what his circumstances were, but also to consider the context - economic, social and environmental - for his life. This window on life in south-west Scotland in the eighteenth century is hardly authoritative and certainly not exhaustive but makes it possible to say what life must typically have been like for Paterson, at home, at work or on his travels, and for his family.

In doing so we can also assess the reliability of the story which has been left to us and try to resolve some of the contradictions thrown up by the main sources on which it based, such as: the motives for Paterson's itinerant lifestyle and what gave rise to it; where he travelled and why; and when and where he died. Addressing these specific points is a third theme of the book.

Finally, there is Paterson's most enduring legacy, even if it is a more morbid one to modern minds - the gravestones and other funereal monuments which he erected and engraved in churchyards and individual burial plots across the region. Very few original stones still exist, even fewer *in situ*, although several have been recut or even reproduced over the years. The evidence of the stones, and other records which suggest where Paterson might once have visited, provide a trail with which to follow the stonemason (or 'stonecutter' as contemporaries labelled his profession) on his travels, albeit in no particular order.

Together with the areas in which we know he lived and worked, the opportunity which this affords us to wander around and learn about some of the quieter and more remote corners of this part of Scotland is, I hope, an enjoyable fourth theme of this book.

These four themes are intended to set Paterson's life in a strong historical, geographical and environmental context. Altogether they should help to bring Scott's literary character into sharper focus and allow us to follow, as it were, more closely in the tracks of Mortality.

CHAPTER ONE

MORTALITY, THE NOVELIST AND THE EXCISEMAN

Old Mortality
In the summer of 1793, in a graveyard in the parish of Dunnotar on the north-east coast of Scotland, there occurred a chance meeting between Robert Paterson, a stonemason known by local people as 'Old Mortality', and the still unknown but aspiring writer, Walter Scott. The event was mentioned briefly years later in a letter that Scott wrote to a admirer[1] and, if true, took place when Paterson was already in his eighth decade and a long way from his home in the hills of Galloway, in south-west Scotland.

In the autumn of 1816, as an established novelist, Scott recalled the event in detail in the opening chapter of *The Tale of Old Mortality*. Scott was staying with his friend, Patrick Murray, at Meigle in Forfarshire and they had travelled over to Dunnotar to view the castle ruins. The stonemason whom they met in the nearby churchyard, according to Scott, was pursuing his lifetime's work of restoring the gravestones and monuments of the Covenanters, an austere religious movement of the seventeenth century.

Using artistic licence, Scott painted the picture of a tranquil summer evening where, amongst "the gentle chiding...of the brook, and the sighing of the wind in the boughs", his peace was disturbed by the occasional "clink of a hammer" in the distance. Upon closer inspection, he came across

> "An old man...seated upon the monument of the slaughtered Presbyterians, and busily employed in deepening, with his chisel, the letters of the inscription..."

The old man's appearance was unusual, he thought.

> "A blue bonnet of unusual dimensions covered the grey hairs of the pious workman. His dress was a large old-fashioned coat of the coarse cloth called *hoddin-grey*, usually worn by the elder peasants, with waistcoat and breeches of the same; and the whole suit, though still in decent repair, had obviously seen a train of long service. Strong clouted shoes, studded with hobnails, and *gramoches* or *leggins*, made of thick black cloth, completed his equipment."

And he was not alone.

> "Beside him, fed among the graves a pony, the companion of his journey, whose extreme whiteness, as well as its projecting bones and hollow eyes, indicated its antiquity."

Scott entered into conversation with the old man, invited him to a local tavern for a drink and teased out of him some ill-tempered views on the state of modern morals and religious observance. He then used the tales which he said Old Mortality gave him as a pretext to hark back to the time of the Covenanters, the backdrop for the tale of 'star-crossed' lovers with which the rest of the novel is concerned. Thus he evoked an atmosphere which was at once redolent of former times - even Paterson's appearance was straight out of the seventeenth century - and timeless, for the character, the materials with which he worked and the monuments transcended the activity of the world beyond and created - however briefly - a haven from it.

The rest of Scott's novel is a fictionalised account of historical events and real characters - a trademark of his writing and a way of portraying a story that will be familiar to modern TV audiences. The character on whom Old Mortality was based was no less real but, to begin with, Scott had few facts concerning his background: in the novel he confessed to not knowing where he was born or even learning his real name. However, the success of the novel helped to fix the figure of the old stonemason, as with so many other characters from Scott's novels, firmly in the popular imagination and in 1829, as part of a new edition of all of his works, Scott revised the introduction to *The Tale of Old Mortality* in order to shed more light on the man, his life and his family.

This new introduction remained the most complete yet concise version of Robert Paterson's life available for almost seventy years and still forms the basis for most other accounts of his life over the last couple of centuries. Any attempt to fill the gaps in the story - to put flesh on the bones, as it were - must therefore start here.

The Exciseman
Scott carried out extensive research for his novels, from personal contacts, old manuscripts and a wide range of reading matter. For the story of Old Mortality, however, he relied largely on just one source of information - as, to a great extent, we still must today - that of Joseph Train, the customs and exciseman who regularly furnished Scott with local tales, traditions and not a few artefacts concerning aspects of Scottish history. Train provided an outline of Paterson's life, just enough for Scott's purposes and just the right amount to intrigue readers of the novel, leaving them curious to learn more about this wanderer, his travels and adventures and the motives for his chosen way of life.

As an outline, therefore, Train's account understandably contained large gaps. However, the material with which he supplied Scott also contained a number of errors, some of them crucial, as subsequent writers have pointed out, as well as an interpretation of Paterson's life which has remained largely unquestioned. The rest of this book aims, as much as is possible at this distance in time, to address the gaps in our knowledge of Paterson's life. In the process, it also aims in a sense to establish whether Train's information could be substantiated by other, objective sources, or whether it stemmed - to whatever degree - from his own imagination.

Train first came to Scott's attention in November 1814 when Scott, visiting his printers in Edinburgh, found newly-printed copies of one of Train's earliest published work, *Strains of the Mountain Muse (Poems, with notes illustrative of traditions in Galloway and Ayrshire)*, being bound up, ready to be despatched. Train was a Supervisor of Excise at Newton Stewart at this time and Scott wrote to him, placing an order for twelve copies of the *Strains* and asking if Train would supply him with more information about local folklore and traditions[2]. This was the origin of a partnership which was to last eighteen years. In return for supplying Scott with information and artefacts, Scott also appears to have helped Train's career a little by putting in a good word here and there.

Joseph Train was born on 6 November 1779 in the Parish of Sorn, Ayrshire. He was apprenticed as a weaver but acquired a love of poetry at an early age and had his first works, entitled *Poetical Reveries*, published in 1806. This followed a stint in the militia – the early nineteenth century equivalent of the Territorial Army - where he found support for his enthusiasm from his commanding officer, a fellow admirer of Burns and another Ayrshireman. Following in Burns' footsteps, Train joined the Excise Department in 1808 being stationed first at Ayr but was transferred to Newton Stewart, in Galloway, in 1813.

Train's duties as an exciseman required him to travel extensively across the south-west of Scotland, including some of the remoter, rural areas of the region. This brought him into contact with people who still lived traditionally, with a rich store of sayings, folk tales and traditions to relate. He wrote them all down for later use and, if there were any particularly interesting antiques to be had, he bought or asked to be given those as well.

This provided Train with enough information to publish *Strains of the Mountain Muse* in 1814 which led, as we have seen, to his introduction to Sir Walter Scott whose fame by this time was widespread.

However, this chance contact also put a temporary halt to Train's literary career. Scott's request to be supplied with notes or anecdotes concerning the history and traditions of Dumfries, Galloway and Ayrshire met an immediate and enthusiastic response, persuading Train to devote much of his life thereafter to supplying Scott with material for his work. In one of his notebooks he wrote:

> "From the day I became acquainted with Sir Walter Scott, the ambition of authorship was superseded by a desire to serve the great novelist".[3]

Charles Dickens, writing the exciseman's obituary many years later, put it more effusively. Train, he said, acknowledging his role in supplying material for Scott's novels,

> "... readily accepted the office of purveyor to his literary majesty. He swept hill, glen and dale, from the Nith to the Irish Sea, from the Ayrshire Border to the Solway, for the rarest flowers of tradition, and laid them at the master's feet."[4]

At least until his retirement, Train therefore lived the literary career he would have preferred vicariously, through Scott. This was an understandable decision given the opportunity which was presented to him and one which was, admittedly, assisted by the need to support his young family. Train's efforts to date made him realise that, for him, a literary career would not have been financially viable.

Over the years, Train supplied Scott with much of the background to his historical novels and perhaps some of the inspiration. In his memoirs[5] of their relationship Train listed the artefacts and curios which he managed to track down and give or send to Scott. These formed an eclectic, not to say esoteric, collection. In 1814, for example, he sent Scott a drinking cup which he was informed "on good authority" had been used by the lepers of King's Carse, a leprosy colony founded by Robert the Bruce. In 1815 he presented Scott with "a Roman battle axe, found in the moss of Cree", "the head of a spear picked up near Merton Hall, in the parish of Penninghame" and the "Antic purse (ie. the sporran) that once belonged to the celebrated freebooter Rob Roy". Occasionally Train cross-referenced his offerings to Scott's novels as in "Ladle of the last resident hangman in Dumfries, mentioned in Waverley novels vol.2, p408".

Later in their friendship he obtained "a black oaken bedstead, well authenticated to have been the principal one in the Castle of Threave and said to have been that of the Black Douglas himself". This latter never reached Scott and neither did the novelist ever receive "The mallet and square used by Old Mortality in his pious work of repairing the martyrs' gravestones... These well-worn instruments", Train added, "have been most kindly placed in my hands by my friend Mr Robert Patterson (sic) of Balmaclellan, the only surviving son of Old Mortality."

Genesis
Concerning the origins of *Old Mortality*, Train described an overnight stay with Scott and his family in Castle Street, Edinburgh in May 1816. This, it appeared, was their first face-to-face meeting. Scott may have been anxious to lay on the hospitality as Train had been left standing in the rain the year before when, due to some misunderstanding, he had made the trek to Edinburgh only to find the novelist away on business. It certainly stuck in Train's memory as he recalled the stay in elaborate terms in his memoirs.

After a good supper the previous night, Scott encouraged Train to pass some time before breakfast in his library which was famously well-stocked, a real treat for the exciseman from the country. What followed is recorded in sufficient detail to make us suspicious of its accuracy, written as it was some seventeen years later, after the novelist's death. In essence, however, it appears that a conversation started around the subject of a full length portrait on the library wall, that of John Graham of Claverhouse, later Viscount Dundee, who was killed at Killiecrankie in 1689, defending the Stuart throne against the forces of William of Orange. As far as Train was concerned, Claverhouse ("bludy Clavers" as he referred to him) was more notorious for leading royal troops against individual and parties of Covenanters in south-west Scotland in the early 1680s, the so-called 'Killing Times'.

According to Train, Scott aired the desire to construct a novel around the figure of Claverhouse, whom he admired for his loyalty to his royal master, as well as having a romantic attachment to the Jacobite cause itself. However, he acknowledged that his proposed theme would have to be carefully handled if he was not to offend Presbyterian susceptibilities which were still prevalent in the south-western counties. Why not, Train therefore suggested, treat the story as emanating from the voice of a supposedly staunch Presbyterian of that period? Why not use the figure of Old Mortality himself? "Old Mortality!" Scott is said to have exclaimed, "Man! Who was he?", apparently forgetting that he had already met him on the occasion described above.

Train briefly recounted the story of Old Mortality to Scott before they went for breakfast and, gauging Scott's interest in the subject, promised to send more information in due course. "Proud of the kind reception I had met with in Edinburgh from Sir Walter", Train concluded, "I returned to Galloway, resolving to use every means in my power to serve him by collecting traditionary (sic) stories of every description but more particularly what related to the Covenanters and to Old Mortality."[6]

The Novelist
Scott's literary debut had been in poetry. He came to prominence with the *Border Minstrelsy* of 1802 - a collection of ballads from the Borders region. This was followed by *The Lay of the Last Minstrel, Marmion* and *The Lady of the Lake*, all long poems often described as 'novels in verse'. However, the novel which was forming in both men's heads would be written hot on the heels of the success of *Waverley, Guy Mannering* and, in the very same month that they met in Edinburgh, *The Antiquary*. They were all part of a series of historically-based novels in prose, a form to which Scott had reverted only two or three years previously.

The series had also, up till now, been published by the firm of Constable. However, even as the last book was coming off the presses, Scott was negotiating for the publication of his next work with the firm of Murray and Blackwood out of pique for Constable's refusal to use Ballantyne's, the firm of printers in which Scott had a sizeable investment.

Tales of my Landlord, which was to be a series of four short novels, was offered anonymously to Murray and Blackwood and, on the basis of the first draft of volume one, *The Black Dwarf*, they accepted enthusiastically. The themes of the succeeding volumes were, however, not decided upon and it is here that Train may have been instrumental in guiding Scott's thinking.

In the end, Murray and Blackwood were disappointed with the final draft of *The Black Dwarf*, with which Scott appears to have lost interest, perhaps because he had moved onto his next project, *Old Mortality*. The latter was apparently written in the space of a few weeks during the autumn of 1816. It rapidly expanded to become volumes two, three and four of the *Tales* and eventually assuaged the concerns of his new publishers. *The Tale of Old Mortality* was published, together with *The Black Dwarf*, on 1 December that year.

On 21 December, Scott wrote to Train in elusive terms, possibly explained by his desire not to be identified as the author of the *Tales*. "...(M)y sincere thanks", he offered,

> "for your very obliging and curious communication from which I have derived both instructions and amusement... you have been uncommonly successful in some most interesting enquiries. You will be surprised to find that Old Mortality has got into print..."

It is not clear what information Scott had received from Train concerning Old Mortality but it was certainly limited, judging by the extent of Paterson's life story which is contained in the first chapter: the bare facts are covered in just one paragraph. His biographer, writing in 1857, said that Train kept his promise to supply Scott with more information concerning Robert Paterson "within a few weeks" adding, however, that the information supplied was from Train's own knowledge of the story rather than any first hand source, such as Paterson's son.[7] In other words, although it is unlikely that Train would not have been aware of Robert junior's existence, he may have decided to improvise as best he could in order to keep up the momentum which he had started. This was to have later implications.

Train, not surprisingly for the novel was enormously successful, had no doubt of his own contribution. One writer has argued that Train "had every reason to exaggerate his own role in inspiring a writer whom contemporaries freely compared with Shakespeare."[8] Despite this, it appears that Train did make a significant contribution at least to the genesis of the novel and supplied Scott with enough information on Paterson, as well as some further background on Claverhouse, to spur the novelist into action. This is acknowledged by two of Scott's biographers, John Gibson Lockhart, his son-in-law, writing a few years after Scott's death[9], but with the benefit of material supplied by Train and while the former exciseman was still alive, and Edgar Johnson, writing in 1970.[10]

Magnum Opus

In 1820, Train was promoted to the grade of Supervisor, one of only seventy such posts in Scotland, and transferred to Dumfries. Scott appears to have been influential in securing the new post for Train which the latter acknowledged in a letter written in 1829 ("...although it is eight years since through your goodness I was first appointed to that station"[11]). He spent six or seven years here, living near the Observatory buildings, now part of the town's Museum, and appears to have enjoyed it enormously being, as he was, more at the heart of matters literary. In 1827, however, he was persuaded, reluctantly, to accept a transfer to Castle Douglas where he lived until his retirement from the Excise.

But as Train's career was experiencing an upturn, the life of his literary master had taken a decided turn for the worse. In 1826, the printing firm of Ballantyne's crashed, taking much of Scott's fortune with it and leaving several large debts. These Scott generously took on, hoping to pay them off through his writing. As part of this effort, Scott was persuaded to prepare a revised edition of his complete works for publication - his *Magnum Opus* he was to call it. Joseph Train was also recruited to provide new details concerning the historical background and characters of the novels and, though he had hardly been inactive up till this point, the letters soon started to arrive more promptly and in greater volume than before.

Fresh information concerning Old Mortality arrived in two batches in the spring of 1829. The first letter was sent by Train on 31 March and formed the basis of Scott's new introduction to the novel which was eventually published in 1830.* As soon as he received it, Scott forwarded the letter to his publisher asking that a copy of the letter be made and "dovetailed into the account of old Paterson as it now stands".[12]

Just over a week later, Scott replied to Train thanking him for his "valued communication (which) arrived in clipping time..."[13] The letter is significant, not just because Scott rarely replied to Train's offerings simply to thank him - to do so would have taken too much time given the volume he received - but because it

---

* Train's letter forms part of the interleaved set of annotations which Scott made to the 1822 edition of his novels when revising the text for the 1830 edition. This was originally kept by Robert Cadell, Scott's publisher, for security but also as proof of copyright, presumably until his death. It then went on its travels for many years until it was acquired by the National Library of Scotland in 1986. The interleaved set of volumes relating to *Old Mortality* is now MSS 23007 & 23008.

was a further example of the efforts which Scott made to advance Train's career whenever he could. In his earlier letter, Train had complained about being passed over for further promotion at work, saying that preference was being given to Englishmen, and blamed the need to work hard to prove himself for a recent delay in sending material to Scott.

Scott needed no further prompting. He told Train that he was expecting a visit from a senior government official in a position of influence over customs and excise and, as Scott recorded in his journal for 18 April, he wrote "to honest Joseph Train desiring he would give me some notion how to serve him with Mr Carr and to take care to make his ambition moderate and feasible".[14] On this occasion, unfortunately, nothing seems to have come of the meeting.

By this time, Train had made contact with Robert Paterson junior, some seventy-three years of age and living in the village of Balmaclellan, about twenty miles north-west of Dumfries. Train's letter of 31 March had been based on a - much shorter - note by Robert junior, as he made clear in his later memoirs, adding in a footnote that he had received from him "several documents in his Father's handwriting, with the Mallet and Square used by him in following his avocation."[15] Of these letters and mementoes none appear to have survived although a leather pocket book found among Old Mortality's possessions upon his death is now in the collection of Dumfries Museum. It contains an unsigned, and undated, pencilled note attesting to its authenticity.

The contents of Robert junior's original letter were fortunately recorded for posterity before it disappeared.* They make interesting reading when contrasted with Train's account as it becomes obvious that Train added significantly to Old Mortality's life story putting a crucial slant on the motives for his behaviour. He also committed a number of errors of fact, including a vital error concerning the location of the old man's burial, as we shall see. Whether this was based on other evidence or not is unclear.

On 12 May 1829 Train wrote again on the subject of Old Mortality in response to Scott's request for more information concerning the so-called 'Napoleon connection', an odd little footnote to Paterson's family history which is dealt with in Chapter Eight. This time Train took the trouble to enclose a longer letter from "Robert Paterson of Dalry" (sic) which described the life of his brother John, Paterson senior's eldest son. In his covering letter, Train also included further anecdotes concerning Old Mortality which Scott evidently thought good enough to add to the end of his new introduction.[16]

---

* See specific references in subsequent chapters and especially Chapter Ten for more on this.

The Final Years

By the time *Old Mortality* was published Scott was already beginning to suffer the effects of the long illness of which he was to die in 1832, before the full series of the *Magnum Opus* had been released. The new edition was nonetheless a complete success and, together with the sale of the copyright upon Scott's death, completely paid off his debts.

In July 1833, as a final contribution to their partnership, Train sent a *Brief Sketch of a Correspondence with Sir Walter Scott commencing in the year 1814* to Lockhart who was writing his father-in-law's biography. Train retired from the Excise in 1836 and eventually resumed his own literary career. *The History of the Isle of Man* was published in 1845 and *Buchanites from first to last* in 1846, the story of a religious sect which had been active in Ayrshire in the middle of the eighteenth century.* He died in 1852 and was buried in Castle Douglas parish churchyard.

There was a genuine academic aspect to Train's work as a collector and antiquarian which has gone largely unrecognised because of his literary pursuits. His biographer, John Patterson, pointed out, for example, that Train's investigative work revealed a Roman presence in Wigtownshire which had not been previously suspected and was only confirmed in the twentieth century. He also gathered evidence for the existence of the 'Deil's Dyke', a series of natural and man-made features dating from the fourth and fifth centuries which runs diagonally north-west/south-east across Dumfriesshire. And a small number of the artefacts which he uncovered are now on display in Dumfries Museum, although most of the original collection appears to have been dispersed over the years.

It is inevitable, however, that Train should be remembered for his role as Scott's researcher and, whatever doubts there may be about his accuracy as an historian, there is little doubt that his instinct for rescuing tales and traditions from obscurity ensured that they survived through the pen of his more famous contemporary. Without implying that their respective talents were in any way comparable, other contemporaries were keenly aware of the symbiotic nature of the relationship between the two men.

Lockhart, in his *Life of Robert Burns*, described Train as "able and amiable" and said that his services to Scott had been "of high importance to him... in the prosecution of his literary labours".[17] A more modern biographer of Burns, Ian McIntyre, nonetheless warned that Train's "main usefulness to Scott had been as a supplier of ballads and old tales from that misty region where the boundary between tradition and legend can be fluid."[18]

---

* The Buchanites were one of several sects which seceded from the established church during the eighteenth century. They were led by a Rev. Whyte who formed an odd alliance with a Mrs Buchan, who claimed the gift of prophecy and spent her time rousing the populace to prayer. Their conduct led them to be hounded out of Ayrshire and, together with 40 followers, they travelled into Dumfriesshire, basing themselves at New Cample, in Closeburn, for a period.

In an obituary of Train written in 1853, Charles Dickens recalled a visit he had paid to Train's house in Castle Douglas late in the previous year, only a month or so before the antiquarian's death. "'He was a tall old man", Dickens remembered,

> "with an autumnal red in his face, hale-looking, and of simple, quaint manners."

Of the house he described a room which was

> "full of antiquities - here a rude weapon of the aboriginal Celt, or one of the conquering Roman; there a baptismal font from Wigton monastery... in the corner was a stately, white-headed yellow staff which belonged to John Knox".

And in a corner, near the staff,

> "was a modern and homely relic - a pair of substantial cloth boots that had been worn by Sir Walter Scott."[19]

Notes

1   Letter to Rev John Carslaw of Airdrie, 22 May 1827 in *Letters of Sir Walter Scott*, vol.10, ed. HJC Grierson
2   *Memoirs of the Life of Sir Walter Scott*, J G Lockhart, vol.II, Edinburgh 1837-8.
3   *Brief Sketch of a Correspondence with Sir Walter Scott commencing in the year 1814*, Joseph Train, 1st July 1833, National Library of Scotland (NLS) MS 3277. This was written and sent to Lockhart, Scott's son-in-law and biographer, following the author's death.
4   From Dickens' 'Household Words' column, reprinted in the *Dumfries Courier* on 26 July 1853.
5   *Brief Sketch...* op cit.
6   Ibid
7   *Memoir of Joseph Train, the Antiquarian correspondent of Sir Walter Scott*, John Patterson (Glasgow) 1857
8   Angus Calder, writing in the introduction to the Penguin edition of *Old Mortality* published in 1975.
9   *Memoirs*, Lockhart, *op cit.*
10 Johnson, Edgar *Sir Walter Scott: the Great Unknown*, Hamish Hamilton, 1970.
11 Train to Scott, 31 March 1829. The letter is contained in Vol.VII of the Interleaved Waverley Novels: *The Black Dwarf & Old Mortality*, MS 23007, Nat/l Library of Scotland
12 *Letters of Sir Walter Scott* Vol.XI, 1828-31, ed. HJC Grierson. Scott wrote to Robert Cadell on 9 April 1829 enclosing "some more information about 'Old Mortality' last night received".
13 *Letters...*, 18 April 1829.
14 *The Journal of Sir Walter Scott*, ed. by W E K Anderson, Clarendon 1972. Scott only kept a journal, or diary, for the last five years of his life.
15 *Brief Sketch...* op cit.
16 Train to Scott, 12 May 1829, contained in *Letters received by Sir Walter Scott*, labelled *Mr Train*, NLS, MS874
17 J G Lockhart, *Life of Robert Burns*, Edinburgh 1828
18 Ian McIntyre, *Dirt & Deity, A Life of Robert Burns*, Flamingo 1995
19 Dickens, 'Household Words', *op cit.*

CHAPTER TWO

BEGINNINGS

Death and Life
Robert Paterson was born in the town of Hawick, Roxburghshire – in the Borders region of Scotland - in 1713. He was also born in 1716. The parish records for both births give "Walter Paterson of Burnflat" as the father. The mother's name is given as Helen Scott in the case of the first birth and Margaret Scott for the second although there is strong evidence that they were one and the same woman.

Writing over a hundred years later, Joseph Train established "on the best authority" that Old Mortality's parents were indeed Walter Paterson and Margaret Scott. The "authority" was Robert Paterson junior but it was not of the best when it came to establishing the date of his father's birth.

The happy consensus at which Train arrived was 1715. The family gravestone in Balmaclellan, erected in 1855 by Thomas Paterson, one of the sons of Robert junior, says that his grandfather died in February 1800 at the age of 88 which puts the year of his birth in about 1712. Paterson's own memorial stone in the cemetery at Bankend of Caerlaverock, which was erected some fifteen years later still, gives the date February 1801 for his burial but no age or birth date.

As late as 1897 the Hawick Archaeological Society, despite claiming to have examined the parish register, unveiled a plaque to Paterson's memory on the house in which he was born giving the date as 1712. The matter was resolved in 1898 by James King Hewison, a Dumfriesshire-based historian, in his excellent, if highly stylised, series of essays, *Chisel Prints of Old Mortality*[1] where he explained the discrepancy.

In both cases, Robert Paterson was baptised on the day of his birth. Of the first child, born on 14 July 1713, parish records say that Paterson had "a son baptised Robert before these witnesses - John Scott *distinctus causa*, called John the Soldier, and Henrie Paterson, carrier, in Hawick". The second record, for 25 April 1716, says that he had "a son baptised, called Robert, before these witnesses - Walter Paterson (gardner) in Hawick and Walter Scott, Beddal". (John Scott was the son of Walter Scott, the parish 'beddal' or beadle and was presumably deputising for his father in 1713 - he inherited the post upon his father's death in 1719. Henrie Paterson was most likely Walter Paterson's brother.)

Hewison says that the likeliest explanation for this double event is that the first child died soon after he was born and that Walter Paterson and Margaret Scott named their next male child Robert as well. We cannot be certain of this as records of deaths, especially children's deaths, were rarely kept and were not, in any case, kept in Hawick where the parish registers are otherwise comprehensive. However, this is the clear implication of the records, supported by the fact that the habit of giving the same name to successive children was not unknown in Scotland at this time. According to the parish records, between 1695 and 1716 the Patersons themselves had at least two Johns, two Walters and, as we have seen, two Roberts. They also had a girl, Helen - their second child - and another boy, Francis, who we know survived into manhood. Together with Robert, the Patersons therefore had at least two surviving children and possibly up to five. It is worth noting in this context that Sir Walter Scott, who was born sixty-five years later, was himself the second child of his parents to bear that name.*

For most families at the beginning of the eighteenth century in Scotland, the stock of names available to recycle was limited, confined for the most part to their own parents' names, or their grandparents or, if they were any different, their own names. Only when a significant number of children survived did 'new' names, not from within the immediate family circle, have to be introduced. This was a feature of a society comprised of small, dispersed and often quite remote communities of whom very few travelled beyond the nearest large village or market town.

Another feature of Scottish society at this time, and one which explained the need to recycle names at all, was the very high infant mortality rate which prevailed. It meant that the tragic pattern of births and deaths which the Patersons witnessed was merely typical of the way of life endured by many families. This in turn was due to the utter poverty and destitution in which many people, and certainly a majority of the peasantry, lived.

The population of Scotland at the beginning of the eighteenth century was about 1.1 million, of whom perhaps ten per cent were in total poverty, according to Henry Grey Graham who based his figures on an appraisal of Andrew Fletcher's *Second Discourse on the Affairs of Scotland*, 1698. "Without adopting Fletcher's numbers as correct" he added, "we may at least accept his vivid picture of the time in which he lived as accurate - one of widespread misery, of abject need or famine".[2]

The country had experienced several years of poor harvests just before and around the turn of the century. The population had hardly begun to recover from them when, in 1709, a bout of prolonged bad weather led once again to the destruction of crops and the death of cattle resulting in famine conditions

---

* In an article in the Transactions of the Hawick Archaeological Society in 1924, entitled 'Old Mortality' by J W Kennedy, the interesting suggestion was put forward that there might have been two *live* Roberts in the family as there were examples of children being given the same name in other families. This seems unlikely and the argument appears to have been put forward to defend the Society's oversight when examining the register.

throughout much of Scotland. The effects of this series of disasters were so devastating that the national population has been estimated to have been up to a third smaller at the end of the first decade of the eighteenth century as it had been at the beginning of the last decade of the seventeenth century.[3]

It was during this period that the Patersons saw at least five children born of whom three seem likely to have died within a year. In fact, the country did not really undergo a steady and sustained rise in population until the middle years of the eighteenth century - even as late as 1740 another severe winter resulted in the death of thousands of animals and the widespread loss of crops.

It was into this poor state of affairs that Robert Paterson was born. Indeed, it seems that there were doubts about even the second Robert surviving as he was baptised on a Sunday, officially the day of mass and not one reserved for other functions of the church, such as weddings, funerals or baptisms. However, had he not been baptised immediately, the ceremony would certainly have been performed the very next day. This was an elementary precaution to ensure that a child, if it died, had at least been received into the church. But there was also a ring of superstition about it.

A belief in the spirit world and its capacity for good or ill still clung on in many parts of the country but particularly in the more remote areas, away from regular contact with churches and schools. "Side by side with belief in the doctrine of the Confession of the Faith", said one commentator, "was the respect for notions whose sources were pagan, or popish or satanic."[4]

In Nithsdale, Dumfriesshire, for example, where Robert would later live, in spite of its strong Presbyterian beliefs the custom was kept well into the eighteenth century, of washing in the Doo Loch, near Penpont, and leaving offerings to cure illnesses and bring good luck.[5] Belief in witchcraft was also still strong throughout the country, and there were incidents of 'witches' being tried and killed as late as the 1730s. (At Cubbox, near Balmaclellan, Galloway, where Robert would later take his family, Elspeth MacEwan was tried and executed for witchcraft in 1700.) In Hawick itself it was still the custom at this time to slaughter a fatted ox following the annual 'land setting' or letting of land by the landowners. In a ritual laden with pagan overtones, the ox was feted on its arrival in the town, being garlanded with flowers and preceded by a piper on its way to the butcher's.[6]

Similarly, in many districts, but more especially in the highland areas, a child was regarded as being at risk from abduction by fairies until it was christened in the nearest church. For this reason, family and friends kept a close eye on it, especially at night, until the christening. Whether or not this belief clung on in Hawick until Robert Paterson's birth, his parents could not be blamed for wanting to ensure that their child was properly baptised in the Christian faith in case this latest child was also lost to them.

The Parish and Burgh

At the time of Robert's birth the parish of Hawick, within which the town sat, was extensive, covering some twenty-four square miles in total. However, the majority of the population lived in or near the town, within the confines of the 'burgh'. According to a statistical account undertaken by William Somerville, the Minister of Hawick from 1732-56, there were about 1800 people in the parish of whom two-thirds lived in the town itself. He counted just "31 steads" or collections of houses in the "landward" part of the parish, outside the burgh.

The latter had received its charter from James Douglas of Drumlanrig in 1537 when it was established as a Burgh of Barony. Since 1686, the lands and title of the Barony of Hawick had been vested in the Duchess of Buccleuch, whose family name was Scott – nearby Branxholme Castle was the family's ancestral home. Hawick Tower, also known as Drumlanrig's Tower, in the centre of town, was another one of her residences and had been redeveloped by her as a comfortable town house as recently as 1702.

Indeed, Anne, the Duchess of Buccleuch, had led a charmed life. She inherited her titles and estates at the age of only eleven and, being one of the most eligible heiresses in the country, was married within a year to James, Duke of Monmouth, a natural son of Charles II and himself only fourteen on his wedding day. Monmouth was to forfeit his titles, and his life, following the failed rebellion against James VII (II of England) in 1685, but Anne was able to keep her Scottish titles, and the rent due from the land that came with them. She remarried, had eight children altogether, and continued to live a life of luxury, remaining a court favourite of successive monarchs, until her death in 1732. An anonymous history of the Buccleuch family records that "Till the day of her death, she continued to keep up the state of a princess of the blood, being attended by pages, served on the knee and covered by a canopy in her room, and no one was allowed to sit in her presence."[7]

Hawick was on one of the three principal north-south routes between England and Edinburgh and so had grown up as a market town, albeit a "poor market town", as one traveller described it just a year before Robert's birth.[8] The burgh had one main street with houses continuous from the West Port, where the road from Carlisle entered over a twin-arched medieval bridge*, to the East Port where the road to Edinburgh left. The market was held on the Sandbed, near the West Port, within the wedge formed by the confluence of the Teviot and Slitridge rivers, and immediately in front of Hawick Tower.

---

* According to the RCAHMS record, a tablet unveiled on the outside of a local shop in 1952 was inscribed: "Near this spot stood the Auld Brig of Hawick, built in the 13th century: Demolished in 1851". The bridge was believed to date back to the reign of Alexander II (1214-1249).

The houses were low, squat dwellings, mainly of one floor and all, with one exception - the Tower - being thatched.* Interspersed with these were relics of earlier and more unsettled times such as the tower or various fortified and castellated houses, "built when strength and solidity were more valued than comfort".[9] The public buildings were the kirk and the Town House or Council Chamber (both thatched). Most of the houses opened straight out onto the street. There were no pavements and there was no water supply. The street was not lit at night and, although most people had retired to their houses by this time, those who ventured out had to light their own way by carrying lanthorns.

The streets, indeed, were so bad that the Council in 1715 required the burgesses - the principal residents of the town - who had "ousteads of houses and tenements of land within the burgh to help and mend the channels and causeways from their respective foordoor (sic) upon each syd of the street to the top rigging of the cassay (causeway)".[10] There were in fact no roads or tracks capable of taking wheeled vehicles for any appreciable length across any part of the parish and so none existed within the parish, a situation which pertained until about 1760.[11] The improvements, at least to the high street, appear to have been carried out by 1721 but there was, in all of this, more than a remnant of the middle ages and of ancient dilapidation, out of which Scottish society was only just beginning to climb.

The Family
Despite this, Robert Paterson was not, by any means, born into the bottom rung of society. His father was a heritor or 'bonnet-laird' as the expression went, in other words a minor landowner, while the family name went back generations within the parish. One of the principal landowners on which the Town Charter conferred rights and duties in 1537 was one Adam Paterson.[12]

The cottage in which Robert was born was called Burnflatt (or Burnflat) and had been acquired by Walter Paterson from his father in 1688. In the title deeds, the property is described as "lying contiguous to the common of Hawick, and bounded by the water of Slitridge on the south, the said common of Hawick on the west, and the burn or strand called Smaile burn upon the north and east parts." It was valued at £40 Scots (about £3 10s sterling) in 1711 and he held it in 'fee blench', ie. at a peppercorn rent, of 1d Scots paid annually "if it bees asked".[13]

The cottage formed part of a collection of houses and adjoining fields - known as a 'steading', 'township' or, in some parts of the country, as a 'fermtoun' - called *Haggisha'*, of which there are several spellings and an equal number of stories

---

* The RCAHMS record for Hawick Tower states that in 1570 the residents deliberately set fire to the thatch to create a smoke cover that allowed them to escape from the advancing English army under the Earl of Surrey. Only the tower itself was left undamaged.

concerning its derivation. One of the more entertaining concerned one Michael Paterson, a former owner of the property, who was said to have given the place its name by virtue of the "Great chieftain o' the puddin-race" which he was wont to serve to his guests on the feasts of Whitsunday and Martinmas. Wilson, in his *History of Hawick*, 1825, wrote:

> "Michael had made a covenant with himself... that whoever were guests at Haggiesha' upon a holiday, whether they might be kings, priests or mendicants, there should be an unity of fare; and that although the liquids might vary to the extent of the different binns in his cellar, the staple or eating commodity should be a gusty, unadulterated and capacious haggis."*[14]

The cottage was still standing in the late 1980s, when it was being used as a stables for a local farm, and was only pulled down following a fire in 1991. The Smaile Burn has also long gone, possibly diverted under the road which now runs through the site. It was on the brow of a steep hill, about a mile south-west of the centre of town, from which it commanded a fine view back over the rooftops of Hawick.†

It was not a large house by today's standards but to Robert Paterson and his family it would have afforded a degree of space and comfort not available to the majority of his neighbours. It was in the middle of a row of buildings, starting with the barns at one end and the cattlehouses at the other. They were all built of stone, albeit probably of dubious construction, and were thatched. Just one door gave access from the muddy yard outside to the living quarters within which would typically be a space about thirty feet long and about fourteen feet wide and split in two - the 'but' and the 'ben'.[15]

The but was the social focus of the farm - it comprised the kitchen, the dining room for the whole house and sleeping quarters for the servant, if the Patersons had one, as well as for their daughter once she had grown a little. The floor would have been of earth and the walls probably unplastered, with no ceiling below the rafters except for shelves to store food. A large chimney would have projected five or six feet out into the room over the cradle grate and benches would have been arranged around it. Beggars might count on a seat by the fire and something to eat in exchange for a story, gossip or the latest news from

---

* One haggis was reputed to have been over three feet in diameter and, hearing of this story in 1786, Robert Burns is said to have elaborated upon it in his 'To a Haggis' by asserting that "Your pin wad help to mend a mill, In time o' need", ie. that the pin holding it together could be used as the spoke for a water-wheel. Another story has it that the skin was later used as the town drum.
† The location of the cottage is today marked by a stone plinth to which is attached the plaque originally fixed to the outside of the property by Hawick Archaeological Society in 1897, announcing 'The Birthplace of Old Mortality', and still with the erroneous dates. It stands at the entrance to a modern housing estate called, more pleasingly, Paterson's Gardens.

abroad. "The but was a crowded, warm, smokey, busy place where everyone connected with the farm was equally welcome, and where discipline and order was kept by the gudewife."[16]

The ben, by contrast, was Walter Paterson and Margaret Scott's private apartment and where they slept with the rest of the children. It was quite likely to have been timber floored and to have had plaster on the walls, a recessed fire and even a wooden ceiling. It would also have been much better furnished than the but with chairs, a table, box beds, and a mirror. There would also have been shelves for books, especially the Bible and other religious books. It was here that Robert Paterson lived until he was about thirteen.

The diet which he shared with his family was poor and monotonous. Virtually the only two agricultural products of farmers at the beginning of the century were oats and barley. Breakfast, lunch and dinner for the Patersons consisted of endless oatmeal, oatcakes, gruel and, occasionally, 'kail greens' which they grew in their own yard. There were very few other vegetables grown or consumed - potatoes were not grown anywhere in Scotland until the second quarter of the century and not commonly until the 1740s. Fresh fruit was a seasonal rarity as was fresh meat. The family would not have been able to afford to slaughter their own animals for meat on demand, but one or two animals may have been killed in the autumn and salted to preserve the flesh over the winter - this would have allowed Margaret Scott occasionally to provide gruel with mutton or beef.

With almost every meal the family drank ale or beer, probably brewed by Walter Paterson himself from oats and heather. There was milk for the children, but very little as the cows were half-starved, and of course water from the stream. Tea, though known, was still a relatively expensive commodity and did not become fashionable until the middle of the century.

All in all, this made for a fairly basic existence and, when one considers that the Patersons were generally better off than many of their neighbours in the parish, it is easier to understand why so much of the population was at the mercy of bad weather, failed crops and disease. But the Patersons were better off, at least in theory.

The Bonnet Laird

As a heritor, Walter Paterson not only had the benefits of the produce of his own land, but could lay claim to a share of the 'Teinds', a proportion of the value of the local produce of the whole parish. In practice, this was not a great amount and was usually paid by tenant farmers for the most part in kind rather than cash, that is in terms of sheep, eggs, poultry or so many 'bolls' of barley, oats or pease. If the Kirk session records are anything to go by, Walter Paterson was certainly not cash rich, at least not around the turn of the century. The records for 1702 show him paying off a debt of a hundred merks (about £5 sterling) for which he had issued a bond.[17]

In return for their privileges, heritors had a number of legal responsibilities to the community, including an obligation to meet the salary of the local minister. The heritors of Hawick, however, were not a particularly generous group of men and, initially at least, Paterson's contribution consisted of just twelve bags of coal to keep the manse warm in winter. In later years he was forced to make a direct financial contribution and when William Sommerville, the then minister, was successful in obtaining a court order to increase his salary in 1735, Walter's contribution climbed to £14 Scots a year.

The heritors' responsibility also ran to the maintenance of the church, the manse and, from 1696 when an Act of Parliament was passed to this effect, they had the additional obligation to pay for the building and maintenance of a schoolhouse and for a schoolmaster's salary. However, what Parliament decreed and what actually happened, particularly in small towns like Hawick, were two entirely different matters.

By the time Robert Paterson was five years old and ready to begin his education, some twenty-five years after Parliament had established the framework for the Scottish system of elementary education, Hawick still did not have a formal schoolhouse for him to attend. Until 1710, indeed, the elementary or English school was held in the church and the churchyard was used as a playground. At that date the English school was evicted to make way for a grammar school and the English schoolmaster was forced to rent a room elsewhere. This had implications for wear and tear upon the church premises. As early as 1683 the Kirk Session records contain a petition from John Purdom, schoolmaster, for a schoolhouse to be built as the church "pews had suffered a considerable loss by scholars breaking the same".[18]

The English School
It was to the English school, at about seven o'clock one morning, in the autumn of 1721, that Robert Paterson was sent to learn to read and write, be taught basic arithmetic and to be given a solid grounding in the scriptures. For this his parents paid a shilling a term plus the cost of materials. Robert, or very likely his father, had also to supply straw for the school room floor - it was unlikely that there would have been much in the way of furniture - and, during the winter, he would have contributed coal or peat for the fire. The school day lasted about ten hours, less in winter when school began at sunrise and ended at sunset, with breaks of an hour in the morning for breakfast and another after midday for lunch.

The schoolmaster was the John Purdom already mentioned: a man who appears to have led the life of an ascetic, had the patience of Job and possessed the stamina of an ox. Aside from Robert's father, he may also have been one of the first major influences on the young Mortality's subsequent way of life.

Purdom's principal claim to fame was that he was wounded in the defence of the town in 1679, when the Covenanter army besieged and took the tower as part of the Pentland Rising, subsequently put down by Government troops. The fact that Purdom resisted the Covenanters does not imply that he took the Government side, merely that he was defending his own community in an area which does not seem to have had strong leanings to the Covenanters. (See Chapter Six for more on the rising and the beliefs of those involved.)

When the Presbyterian church regained the ascendancy in 1689, the existing minister was ousted from his post but it is significant that Purdom not only kept his position as schoolmaster but was also asked to deputise as the town's minister until a new appointment could be made, implying that he retained the respect both of the community and of the church authorities. In the end he filled the post for two years, until the Reverend Alexander Orrock took up the appointment in 1691.

How Purdom was able to scrape together an income for himself and his wife is not entirely clear. The income from school fees was meagre and irregular. School attendance was not compulsory and many parents kept their children away from school when there were jobs to do around the house and farm, retaining a proportion of their fees into the bargain. In effect, this meant that few children attended school during the summer or once they were able-bodied. The average length of school attendance for boys was about four years and perhaps half that for girls.

Several requests were put to the town council and the Kirk Session, the governing bodies for the burgh and parish of Hawick, respectively, to provide Purdom with a salary. This suggests that, even when the request was agreed, the money was either not paid or that it later ceased to be paid. In 1703, for example, when Purdom had already been teaching for thirty-four years, a request was put to the town council for fifty merks a year (about £2 10/- sterling) for "the encouragement of ane flourishing school and ane able and weell qualified schoolmaster, for learning and educating of children and for presenting in church upon Sundayes..." Although it appears to have been agreed, Purdom was forced to repeat the request in 1710 when, to add insult to injury, the establishment of the new grammar school was found to have deprived him of a number of older pupils and hence a proportion of his fees.

To supplement his income Purdom, like so many of his counterparts in other towns and villages across Scotland, took on other duties. Thus we find that he was also the clerk to the Kirk Session, probably the registrar of births and marriages, and acted as the precentor or reader at masses. Indeed Sunday was a very busy day for him as church attendance, unlike school, was compulsory and all children of school age were expected to meet in the school for the purpose of reading the scriptures, after which they were marched off to church - which lasted until the afternoon - then back again to be quizzed on what they had learnt.

Purdom appears to have stopped short of acting as the parish gravedigger, but this was not unheard of in other areas. In 1710, in response to his renewed request for a salary, the Session agreed to pay him £18 Scots (thirty shillings sterling) a year for his church duties. The council also paid him 1 shilling a quarter to teach the children of the poor who could not otherwise afford fees.

Already in his late seventies when he began to teach Robert, Purdom was eighty when he retired at the end of 1723 after fifty-four years as the town's schoolmaster. It is easy to imagine the old man in his last two years of teaching, trying to keep order in the classroom, while reinforcing the lessons of the scriptures, by reminding his young pupils of the deeds of the Covenanters and what they stood for and, with little prompting, re-enacting the siege of Hawick Tower.

When Purdom retired he was obliged, together with his wife, to find new accommodation outside the schoolroom. As a measure of the respect in which he was held, and in recognition of his service to the community, the Session in 1724 granted him ten shillings a year to cover the rent for the rest of his life. The impression left by this relatively generous act was, unfortunately, rather spoilt by the statement which followed it in the Kirk Session minutes. It stressed that this action was not to be seen as a precedent and was, in any case, not likely to cost the Session very much as "Mr Purdom their clerk, being an old man (was) not likely to be long a burthen to them". In fact Purdom died exactly two years later.

The Grammar School

It is not known how long Robert Paterson stayed at school but it is a safe assumption that, within a year of Purdom's retirement as the English schoolmaster, the eight-year old would have passed from there to the grammar school, at least for a couple of years more. The latter, as we have seen, was held in the church and would continue to be so for the duration of Robert's stay in Hawick. St Mary's Church was, and the latest building still is, situated in a lofty and prominent position in the town, atop a natural hillock which rises behind the castle in the 'V' formed by the confluence of the Slitridge and Teviot rivers. It would have been visible to the young Paterson from the moment he left home in the early morning to descend the hill into town.

Here, in addition to receiving instruction in the more basic subjects, Robert would have picked up a smattering of Latin. Some of the phrases he learnt as a result were put to good use later, on gravestone and other monumental inscriptions, their meaning no doubt reinforced by the occasion he had to play amongst the memorial tablets within, and the gravestones surrounding, the church in Hawick. For this classical instruction Walter Paterson paid an extra two shillings a quarter. Robert's father also contributed to the salary of the grammar school teacher, one Mr James Anderson. Anderson had only recently - since 1722 - been appointed but was to stay in post until 1746, by which time a proper schoolhouse had also been built. These two breakthroughs in educational provision in Hawick were not unconnected.

When the Reverend Alexander Orrok died in 1711 he left the equivalent of over £500 sterling in a bequest intended to be used to provide and maintain a grammar school such as already existed in the nearby towns of Jedburgh and Selkirk. Before dying, and with remarkable *sang-froid*, he made clear his intentions to the assembled heritors of the parish, rebuking them for failing to provide for such a facility themselves, but also pointing out the opportunity which now existed for them to make amends by appointing and meeting the salary of a grammar school teacher in the expectation that he would soon have a building to occupy.

The heritors agreed to this deal which bound them to pay a salary of "200 merks Scots money" yearly (about £10 sterling, the legal maximum teacher's wage at the time) for a two-term year consisting of Whitsuntide and Martinmas. They subscribed in varying amounts according to the rental value of their lands, such that Walter Paterson of Burnflat subscribed the sum of 9/2d "offering and corresponding to the sum of £40 as my valued rent of the said lands".[19]

Although the heritors kept up their end of the bargain, a suitable property for a school house was not found until 1724 when a building was left to the community in the will of a local landowner. The building, though ideally located on the Sandbed, behind the town market, was derelict and the refurbishment works were not completed until 1732, some years after Robert had left Hawick.

The Kirk

The school was the principal forum in which Robert and his peers received moral instruction, at least for a significant period of his life. As we have seen, however, it was also inextricably bound up with the other major source of social strictures in Scottish society at this time, the church or kirk. The historical and philosophical underpinnings of the Church of Scotland are examined within Chapter Six, but the important thing to understand is the extent to which it pervaded almost every aspect of daily life at the turn of the eighteenth century, for good or ill, and therefore influenced Robert's upbringing. Only in the final decades of the century, in tandem with the improvements in social and economic life in Scotland, did the church relinquish its influence on individuals and everyday life and attain a more secular outlook.

The system of Scottish education was itself a development of John Knox's teachings. It was a vital part of a Christian society because, like Calvin and Luther, he believed that children were born wicked and that the purpose of education was to prepare children "for the business of life and the purpose of eternity".[20] Outside of school the church continued to regulate the boy's and, later, the man's affairs. On Sundays, Robert had not only to attend mass in the morning and afternoon, with Sunday school before and after, but was also expected then to return straight home and stay indoors, in silent contemplation, for the rest of the day. Only in the evening, around the Sunday dinner, could Robert and his family finally relax and even then they were expected to reflect on the day's lessons.

To help them in their contemplations, the Patersons, in common with many Scottish families, had a standard if narrow selection of reading matter. On the shelves in the ben were a Bible, a Confession of the Faith, and a volume of Rutherford's *Letters*, a series of instructions for life which were a Covenanting favourite. Other authors whose works Robert was likely to have had access to as he grew older were Knox, Bunyan, Boston and Wodrow whose *Cloud of Witnesses*, published in 1714, provided contemporary, if rather fanciful, accounts of the lives, and especially the deaths, of the Covenanting martyrs. It was also an indispensable guide to the locations of their graves. Travellers would also hawk round towns and villages pamphlets with not quite so lofty titles, such as *The prophecies of Peden*, the *Life of Sir William Wallace* and *The ravishing, dying words of Christina Ker, who died at the age of ten* as well as various songs and ballads.

The significance of these works, apart from their likely influence on the young Paterson, was that they provided evidence of a degree of literacy in Scottish society in the 1720s, at least among the lower middle class and above, which is remarkable for the time and in view of the preoccupation with survival which many households were only just escaping. It is important not to exaggerate this fact - literacy levels in general were probably no higher than thirty-five to forty per cent - but the advances made in this respect were clearly a positive aspect of the church's influence.

Another was the attention which the church paid to the condition of all its parishioners, not just those who paid the salaries and filled the coffers each week. As we have seen, the Kirk Session in Hawick was careful to ensure that the children of the poor received instruction as much as the rest. It went further than this, ensuring that the poorest families had food, medicine and clothes, were housed and had a decent funeral. The Kirk session records for 1711-25 show that, in Hawick, the Sunday services collected at least £3-4 Scots a week, or more than £200 a year, of which over half was dispensed straightaway in alms.

The Kirk Session also lent money, sometimes on the strength of pawned articles. This was a more traditional feature of Scottish rural society in the first half of the century than the second and was especially prevalent in more remote areas where banks or similar institutions were not to be found. We have already seen how Walter Paterson availed himself of this facility in 1702. In addition, the Session regulated begging, making local people, whom it knew to be in need, eligible to receive alms while encouraging others, collectively referred to as 'creeples', to leave town, sometimes by force and sometimes by making them discreet payments.

And then there was the church service itself, every Sunday without fail on pain of public censure or fine. The only acceptable excuses for missing church were illness or by "reason of the waters", ie. if the roads were flooded and could not be forded. The first bell was at eight o'clock in the morning, calling the faithful to prayer. By the time of the second bell, at nine o'clock, they were to be assembled in the church, ready to hear the reader - usually the schoolmaster - recite the scriptures. At ten o'clock the third bell rang and the minister entered the pulpit to conduct the rest of the service. This consisted of a series of devotional exercises and the preaching of the Word. At twelve-thirty or so there was a break for lunch of about an hour.

The afternoon consisted of more of the same without the sermon. Before starting his service, the minister bowed in succession to the principal heritors in the church. The order in which he did so was a matter of great jealousy among the heritors who then stood up and reciprocated, thus confirming their status. Walter Paterson was in a group of about a dozen heritors who were among the last to be acknowledged.

The downside of this recognition was that the Patersons could not escape notice if they failed to attend, indeed they probably paid for the privilege by hiring their pews each Sunday thus guaranteeing a seat. The rest of the congregation stood, sat on the floor or brought their own stools each week as seats, in fact space, in the church was at a premium. Although the church building had undergone repairs in 1713, it was structurally unsound and too small for the congregation on the majority of Sundays. On feast days, when attendance was expected to be especially high, a tent would be erected in the church grounds, the additional expense being justified by the above average collection which was made.

The majority of parishioners put up with these conditions - which in many cases were not much worse than those to which they were accustomed at home - out of a combination of duty and tradition, at least until morals became more lax, and comfort more keenly desired, later in the century. However, they also did so because, by attending church they were able to catch up on the latest news of home and abroad, which was delivered from the pulpit, and the latest parish gossip, which they heard from their friends and relations while standing amongst the gravestones before the service began and during the lunch break.

The Patersons probably welcomed this time as much as anyone, living, as they did, slightly out on a limb on the edge of town while, for Robert, the graveyard was already becoming a home from home. And as they passed their time so sociably, church elders took it in turns to scour the town and take a note of who was not attending, more especially if they were to be found in the tavern instead.

On the serious side, the elders had a duty to report on scandals and misdemeanours which came to their attention. They were not necessarily regarded as snoops, merely prying on their neighbours. In the eyes of the church, overlooking a sin was to connive at it and, as one commentator put it, "had a tendency to harden a sinner in his iniquity".[21] Thus armed with the evidence of their own eyes and the tittle tattle of their friends the church elders and the heritors - because there was in truth not much difference between the two groups of men - would convene as the Kirk session after church to compare notes. Much of what they discussed was trivial yet detailed. It included instances of drunkenness, loud or lewd behaviour, accusations about illicit sex or gambling and other matters for which the culprits would be summoned to be interrogated and, if appropriate, made to exonerate themselves publicly in church the very next Sunday.

The Ministers
At the heart of all this activity was, of course, the minister himself. The incumbents in Hawick were all intelligent and educated men, though this did not stop them from conniving in the more intrusive aspects of the church's efforts to enforce its moral code. Obviously, they did so out of the same sense of duty which they imposed on the church elders and parishioners in general and, having done so, had therefore to conform to the very same expectations themselves.

In 1712 the right of 'patronage' was restored to the appointment of ministers (the right of local heritors, rather than the kirk session, to appoint the minister, something which the Covenanters had fiercely opposed) which obliged them in addition to have one eye at least to the prejudices of local heritors and therefore to keep a lid on local disorder and any appearance of moral lassitude. But there was also a pecuniary consideration to bear in mind, as those found guilty of misdemeanours could equally be fined, a course of action which brought in an increasing proportion of the church's revenue as the century wore on.

It is this last point which gives a clue to the wider role of the minister in the town's affairs. As important as his position as guardian of the town's morals was his role in ensuring that the parish was properly administered, and here times were already beginning to change, with the emphasis on practicality and efficiency. The Reverend Orrok was one of the last of the generation of Church of Scotland ministers to have actually suffered for his beliefs, having been imprisoned in Edinburgh during the anti-Covenanter repression of the 1680s. As we have seen, he did not hesitate to inform local heritors of their duties and his legacy of published sermons, which runs into volumes, tells us that he was equally concerned with the interpretation, as well as the application, of church law and scripture. In several day-to-day matters, however, he had let things slip.

When Orrok died, the heritors and other chief residents of Hawick looked for someone with the experience and determination to make changes. In fact they had to look no further than the neighbouring parish of Wilton where the local minister, Robert Cunningham, had acquired a good reputation during his eighteen-year ministry. Cunningham had graduated from Edinburgh in 1689, when the Glorious Revolution was sweeping away old enmities, and had few of the concerns with doctrinal hair-splitting which had pre-occupied his predecessor in Hawick.

After some bitter exchanges between the good people of Hawick and those of Cunningham's existing parish, and an appeal to the synod, he was duly poached. Walter Paterson was one of the petitioners for his transfer to Hawick where the only note of dissent came from a small number of churchgoers who were concerned that Cunningham's soft voice might not be heard from where they sat. Otherwise he took up his new post in June 1712 and immediately set about with a new broom.

During his ten-year ministry, Cunningham appointed eleven new church elders, taking their numbers from eight to nineteen and, in a trend which was not unconnected, exacted fines against sins with renewed enthusiasm. He further increased church revenues by such means as erecting and hiring out new church pews and extended the practice of hiring out 'mortcloths' for funerals.

All of which was useful to the Kirk Session as Cunningham also ordered repairs to the church, at a cost of £47 sterling, and decided that a new manse was required as the old one was, on the authority of the builders appointed to assess the situation, on the point of collapse. This cost the parish a further £75 sterling.

He was also supportive of the cause of education, presiding over the appointment of a new grammar school teacher and, eventually, an assistant who together used the church itself for lessons. Of his character, a local historian commented that he had "a keen eye on every misorder and abuse, was instant in season and out of season in getting things put right".[22] Cunningham was the minister who baptised Robert Paterson and, though Robert would probably have had little day-to-day contact with him, he was the minister who presided over church services when Robert was first old enough to attend and to pay attention.

When Robert Cunningham died, in 1722, he was replaced by his assistant, Charles Telfer, who had been engaged when it became clear that the minister's health was failing. Telfer was even less in the mould of the old, Covenanting preachers than Cunningham, having "scrupled" over signing the Confession of Faith - a requirement for becoming a minister - for seven years, according to his biographers[23], before taking the plunge. He had also graduated from Edinburgh and apparently appealed to the intellectual pretensions of his parishioners for he peppered his sermons with asides and quotations from a number of the eminent thinkers of the day, including the London 'literati'. So much so, in fact, that he was later called to account for the religious significance of one or two of his literary allusions to the church presbytery in Jedburgh. Despite this, and after only a short trial period, Telfer was ordained as the new minister in January 1723 "by unanimous consent and desire of ye heritors, elders and householders"[24] demonstrating once again Hawick's independent streak in church matters.

Taking Stock

Telfer continued in post until 1732 by which time Robert had left Hawick to take up an apprenticeship. According to Hewison, he was thirteen when he left which was about the time most young people began to seek gainful employment, leaving home if necessary. If he had been a scholar, which he evidently was not, he would have left home to begin at university at about the same age.

"Of the boy's early days on the banks of the Smaile and of the Slitridge, and his tricks in the orchards of Burnflatt," laments Hewison, "nothing is known"[25]. Well, perhaps so and perhaps not. As this chapter has attempted to show, we can piece together Robert's beginnings, his family circumstances, and some aspects of his immediate environment as well as gaining a fairly good impression of his daily routine as he grew up.

Some of the principal personalities in his early life are also evident and add to the other list of significant influences which we can, admittedly with some hindsight, begin to connect to later events. Of the influences, the most important is probably the fact that Robert had an impoverished upbringing. By contemporary standards, he had not suffered absolute poverty or destitution but, particularly in his infancy, his family's standard of living was probably not much higher than the great mass of the population. In his daily life on the farm, at school and in church he would have witnessed and shared in the ethos of a community which subsisted at best.

This experience would probably have given Paterson an appreciation of the value of money, and a desire not to squander valuable resources. It would also have made him acutely aware of, and perhaps have inured him to, death and the rituals which surround it. This was not just because of the dead siblings who had preceded him, but also because, from the age of seven or eight, he played routinely among the burial plots of former friends and neighbours, including a former teacher and minister.

Although Hawick and its residents do not appear to have been overly zealous in their religious affiliations and observances, the young Robert would also have been deeply immersed in the history and doctrine of the church, even if he was not yet conversant with every detail of the schisms of the seventeenth century or the life of every martyr. He would certainly have had a very moral upbringing and understood and had a respect for the role of the church in society which was, if his father's attitude was anything to go by, probably a pragmatic one at this stage. He was also able to read and write with a high degree of literacy and, through his family, had an appreciation of the importance of tradition.

None of which singled Robert out as greatly different from the majority of his contemporaries, at least not individually or immediately. But Robert was long-lived and as the century progressed, and Scottish society became more wealthy, bringing in its wake changes in attitudes, these characteristics and values would take on a greater significance.

Notes

1 Hewison, J K, *Chisel prints of Old Mortality*, collected from *The Dumfries & Galloway Standard*, 23 March 1898 and succeeding months.
2 *Social Life in Scotland in the 18th Century*, Henry Grey Graham, A&C Black, 1937. TC Smout, in his *A History Of The Scottish People 1560-1830*, Collins 1969, put the population at the time of the Union (1707) at a million based on estimates made by Sir John Sinclair, general editor of the *Old Statistical Account* of 1792-97.
3 HC Graham, *Social Life, op cit.*
4 HC Graham, *Social Life, op cit.*
5 Old Statistical Account (OSA) for the Parish of Penpont, Dumfriesshire, 1793
6 *Hawick Kirk, 1711-25*, J J Vernon (reprinted from the Hawick Express, 1900)
7 From an unattributed article, written around 1884, which is provided to guides at Drumlanrig Castle.
8 Paton, in his *History of the Insurrection in 1715*. He described Hawick as "belonging to the Buccleuch, at whose house the English Lords, with their relations, took up their abode."
9 Vernon, *op cit.*
10 ibid
11 ibid
12 Hawick Town Charter 1537. The landowners of the burgh had also to keep an oil lamp burning in the church for the wellbeing of the Douglas family.
13 Hewison, *op cit.*
14 Wilson, R, *The History of Hawick*, Hawick, 1825.
15 *A History of the Scottish People 1560-1830*, T C Smout, Collins 1969
16 ibid
17 Hawick Kirk Session Minutes, January 1702
18 Cited in *Hawick and its Old Memories*, James Wilson, 1858.
19 Letter from Duchess of Buccleuch and the heritors of Hawick contributing to the schoolmaster's salary, 6 September 1711, Buccleuch Muniments, National Archives of Scotland.
20 Smout, op cit.
21 Vernon, op cit.
22 ibid
23 'Fasti Ecclesiae Scotticanae', 1917.
24 Hawick Kirk session minutes, 22 November 1722
25 Hewison, *op cit.*

CHAPTER THREE

INTO EMPLOYMENT

Roads and Bridges
Sometime in the summer of 1729, at the age of thirteen, Robert Paterson left home in the company of his older brother Francis to become apprenticed as a stonemason. The pair headed south-westwards, towards the parish of Lochmaben in Annandale, Dumfriesshire, on a journey of around thirty-five miles by the shortest route.

As mentioned in the previous chapter, good quality roads did not exist in Scotland at this time. Indeed, the 'roads' between towns were in reality footpaths or tracks formed largely from the passage of feet and hooves, not by human labour, and varied in width and quality depending on proximity to market towns. In his *Drove Roads of Scotland*, ARB Haldane confirmed that in 1723, only six years earlier, "the roads of Scotland outside the main towns were little more than tracks quite unsuited for wheel traffic which was, in consequence, practically non-existent."[1] Travel therefore almost invariably involved walking or riding on horseback. As late as 1734, there were recorded as being only four horse-drawn carts in Dumfries, the largest town in the region to which they were travelling, two for hire and two in private use.[2]

The responsibility for the repair and upkeep of roads originally lay with justices of the peace who were empowered to call upon local landowners and their tenants to provide the necessary labour for a fixed number of days per year. In practice this power was not used regularly enough, nor was the available labour sufficient in any case, to make up the roads to the necessary standards. In the late seventeenth century the Commissioners of Supply, whose chief priority - and therefore motivation - was the collection of taxes, took on the responsibility at a county level. The Commissioners very quickly realised the benefits of allowing landowners to 'commute' the labour required of them in favour of cash payments. In this way a county fund could be created with which the necessary labour could be purchased for individual works according to their priorities.

To begin with, the Commissioners' priorities lay in bridge building, as the following minute records:

> "At Dumfries, 6th day of August 1717 - ... the Commissioners of the said shyre (considered) that the bridges and high wayes in this shyre are very much decayed and almost impassible, to the great detriment and hinderance of travellers and commoners and that there are several places within the shyre where there will be a necessity for the making of bridges..."[3]

The general lack of bridges meant that, in addition to thinking about the length of the journey and the overall quality of the path they intended to take, travellers had also to consider where and how they could more easily cross major rivers, such as at fords or via settlements built around bridges. The latter would also have opened up more opportunities for food and shelter along the way although this would have been less of a consideration for two young men travelling on a budget. The brothers would probably have been carrying their own provisions: perhaps some oatmeal to mix with water along the way and possibly some bread and cheese and even an onion. Very likely they would have carried their own blanket for the night, in the hope that they could pull it over them and sleep in someone's barn or, at worst, in the lee of a sturdy wall on a warm evening.

Aside from formal paths and roads, travellers of this era would also have been familiar with and could have followed drove roads, the network of cross-country routes created by the feet of cattle being driven to market. Drove roads went essentially from north to south in Scotland, based on the tradition of moving highland cattle down to the markets of the central belt, such as Crieff or Falkirk, then onto border fairs - or 'trysts' as many were known – such as those held several times a year in Hawick. The exceptions were the drove roads that served the southern uplands of Galloway and Dumfriesshire, in the south-west, and which converged on the market at Dumfries. As an adult, Robert would make use of these roads in years to come.

From the border towns the animals were driven to English markets such as Carlisle or Newcastle, exiting through a small number of tightly regulated customs points along the border itself. They finished up in many cases on the rich grazing lands of Norfolk or Suffolk where they were fattened up for the London markets.

The droving tradition in Scotland dated back to the middle ages but crossing the border region to access the English market was not an attractive proposition until the Union of the Crowns in 1603. Prior to that, constant wars between the two countries and the lack of a fixed border in places led to a general lawlessness which was exploited by a number of powerful families to poach land and possessions on either side. Cross border droving certainly took place but largely due to rustling of cattle rather than legal transactions. To avoid the destruction of property, the theft of their goods or the threat to their own lives the members of lesser families had either to support the stronger clans with men and arms or pay for their own protection.

Once relations between Scotland and England had improved and the border had stabilised, trade between the countries also increased, not least in in cattle and sheep. Scottish farmers saw the opportunities of accessing a market that was four times bigger, and more prosperous, than their own. The activity grew still further following the formal union of Scotland and England in 1707 and the development of a legal and financial framework for it and would continue to grow through the eighteenth century. Even by 1729 the numbers of cattle passing through or along routes within just a few miles of Hawick could be counted in their thousands each year.

The drove roads thus created could be twenty or thirty yards wide and, between the markets to the north and the customs points to the south there were a number of well established routes. They exploited gaps in the ranges of hills which ran west to east through the border region and followed the natural contours of river valleys or flat moorland terrain. One such, known as the Minchmoor Drove Road, ran from north of Selkirk down through Hawick and Liddesdale towards the English border at Bewcastle and was used by one of the principal characters in Sir Walter Scott's short story *The Two Drovers* (1827). The drovers who oversaw these cattle journeys were a particular breed of men, Scott said:

> "The highlanders in particular are masters of this difficult trade of driving, which seems to suit them as well as the trade of war. It affords exercise for all their habits of patient endurance and active exertion. They are required to know perfectly the drove roads which lie over the wildest tracts of the country, and to avoid as much as possible the highways which distress the feet of the bullocks."[4]

Scott's description of the droving journey itself implied a perfect symbiosis of animal and nature and adequately summed up the factors which would have determined the route that Robert and his brother took:

> "on the broad green or grey track... the herd not only move at ease and without taxation but, if they mind their business, may pick up a mouthful of food by the way."

A Choice of Routes

The main source of evidence that we have for the alternatives available to the Patersons is General Roy's Military Survey of Scotland which covered most of the country in comprehensive fashion between 1747 and 1755. The lowlands, including the border region, were surveyed in the last three years of that period. The survey was commissioned in the wake of the Jacobite Rebellion of 1745 when government forces found themselves hampered by the lack of accurate knowledge of the Scottish terrain while pursuing Bonnie Prince Charlie's army.

Although produced more than twenty years after their journey took place, when increased traffic might have altered the specific paths or roads that the brothers took, the resulting maps[5] showed their parents' home at Burnflatt, just outside Hawick, and suggest three traditional routes that could have taken them from there to their destination. All three routes were redolent with the centuries of history in which the region was steeped.

The first route headed due west from Hawick, through rough country, towards the hamlet of Ettrick then turned south, through the remote and high-sided valley of the Ettrick Water to its source at Ettrick Head. Here the brothers would either have climbed through a pass below Bodesbeck Law, one of a range of 2,000-foot plus peaks, to descend towards Moffat, in Annandale, or skirted the base of Loch Fell and continued south along a broad moorland ridge to the settlement of Wamphray. The former route was slightly longer but followed a well-trodden drove road which, from Moffat, joined the old Carlisle road. This was a long-established road of (relatively) good quality that ran south to Lockerbie, within two or three miles of Robert and Francis' intended place of work.

The path via Wamphray, which eventually joined the Lockerbie road, was used more by human traffic but is thought to have had ancient origins: just north of Wamphray it crossed another drove road where a tiny medieval church and, before that, a stone cross would have offered a place of prayer to travellers until late in the seventeenth century.* Part of the base of the cross, carved with a dragon motif, can still be seen over the entrance to the Victorian parish church, further down the path. This western route would have been entirely feasible but, overall, was the longest – at up to fifty miles, depending on the route taken - and the most strenuous.

The second option would have taken the brothers due south initially, following the valley of the Teviot Water, one of the two rivers which converged on Hawick. After Teviot Head they had to cross the watershed, several miles of bleak moorland with a choice of narrow valley paths, before entering the Ewes valley and descending to Langholm. The path they would have followed was also used mainly by people on foot or horseback but was crossed by a number of drove roads taking cattle to the eastern border with England.

As with all the options, the countryside through which they passed was largely devoid of habitation, an enduring legacy of the border disputes of the middle ages, except for communities huddled around fortified tower houses, of which Drumlanrig's Tower in Hawick was a prime example. The brothers would have passed a handful more of these on the road to Langholm, the most notable being Branxholme, a prominent five-storey tower house situated on the west bank of the Teviot very soon after leaving Hawick.

---

* The Old Statistical Account for Dumfriesshire, Wamphray Parish, 1793 says the church and other buildings around it were at Braefield but had already been demolished by this date. In conversation with the author, the owner of nearby Laverhay Farm confirmed the existence of the site which is marked on a deed map in his possession. The drove road ran from Boreland in Dryfesdale to Moffat and was used by a local farmer until late in the 20th century once a week to walk into town for band practice.

Branxholme had been in the ownership of the Scotts of Buccleuch since the middle of the fifteenth century and during the following 150 years suffered greatly from the vicissitudes of the Anglo-Scottish disputes of the period. It was besieged, stormed and damaged at least twice before being completely destroyed by English forces in 1570 – gunpowder was apparently used to ensure the job was done properly.[6] The Scotts held the title of Warden of the Middle March (in theory guardians and enforcers of the border) at this time and so were a target for invading forces. However, they were also by definition one of the dominant families of the region and often gave as good as they got.

The property was ordered to be rebuilt, with twin towers, by Sir William Scott of Buccleuch and was completed in 1576, two years after his death. With minor additions, this would have been the building known by Robert Paterson. Sir William's son, Sir Walter Scott (no relation), was the "bauld (bold) Buccleuch" of the border ballad *Kinmont Willie*, edited and collected together with other narratives by his later namesake in *The Minstrelsy of the Scottish Borders* (1802).

The ballad tells the daring, and true, story of the rescue of William Armstrong, a supporter of the Scotts, from Carlisle Castle in 1596. The house was also the setting for the poem, *The Lay of the Last Minstrel* (1805), in which Sir Walter Scott, the author, recounted the more fictionalised story of Baron Henry of Cranston and his attempt to secure the hand of Lady Margaret of Branksome Hall. The tower house still stands today but boasts substantial modern wings, added by the fifth Duke of Buccleuch between 1790 and 1837.

Langholm, had the boys travelled this way, was smaller than Hawick – with a population of less than 500 in the town and just over 1000 in the surrounding parish – but would otherwise have reminded Robert of home with its confluence of rivers: in this case the Ewes, along which valley they would have arrived; the Esk, which continued south to form part of the border with England; and the Wauchope, which drained peat bogs to the south-west, the direction in which they would now turn. They would have entered the town over the medieval, three-arch bridge spanning the Ewes and walked along its single street of about sixty houses and shops plus parish church that followed the course of the Esk.

The whole scene, according to the antiquarian Walter MacFarlane, who visited and recorded his impressions only three years earlier, "gives the most agreeable prospect to strangers."*[7] The only thing missing would have been the tower house: the town had once been the power base of the Armstrong family but their

---

* Reaching the town one evening three quarters of a century later, Dorothy Wordsworth had a similar impression. She said "The town as we approached, from a hill, looked very pretty, the houses being roofed with blue slates, and standing close to the river Esk, here a large river, that scattered its waters wide over a stony channel. The inn neat and comfortable - exceedingly clean: I could hardly believe we were still in Scotland." (*A Tour in Scotland*, 1803)

former stronghold had long fallen into ruin and had been demolished only four years earlier.[8]

Langholm was just under halfway to their destination, following this route, and would have made a convenient stopping point. Like Hawick, the town was a focus for droving and the cattle trade – as well as a strong local tradition of farming sheep for wool – was exploited by some half a dozen fairs each year. As a result, the town boasted several inns and guest houses.[9] Whether Robert and Francis stayed overnight or not, however, for the next stage of their journey they would have turned west about half way down the high street and forded the Esk to find their road on the opposite bank.

After following the meandering Wauchope south-west for five or six miles to its source, the brothers would have had to cross a wide, barren stretch of moorland, dissected by minor burns. Their only distraction, had they wanted it, would have been to note the number of mineral wells which the area boasted. According to MacFarlane, writing in 1726, there was a local chalybeate spa (iron salts) which attracted visitors across the region because its waters were reputed to be a "great deobstruent Diuretick, Antiscorbutick and a cooler in the hectic fever."[10]

After this, they would have descended into the delightful-sounding valley of the Water of Milk. According to tradition, the name was based on a corruption of the Latin *mel* (honey), a reference to beekeeping by local monks in the middle ages. Further evidence for the antiquity of the area lay in the remains of a prehistoric stone circle, known as the 'Seven Brethren', through which their path would have continued on its descent to Lockerbie. Whether the brothers would have understood the significance of the stones is doubtful, however, as archaeology was in its infancy and even major prehistoric sites like Stonehenge and Avebury had barely been surveyed. They were believed to have been built by the Romans or possibly by Iron Age druids but were often associated by locals with fairy stories, pagan rituals or even satanic rites: all anathema to the Presbyterian church but, as described in the previous chapter, all part of contemporary society's schizophrenic adoption of formal religion and informal beliefs.

Altogether this route would have involved some forty-five miles of walking which the brothers could have covered in two long days.

The third route that Robert and Francis could have taken was the most direct and therefore shortest and most likely. The fact that it went through one of the least populated parts of the region was probably not a major consideration given their likely self-sufficiency and the overall length of the journey.

Similar to the first route, the brothers would have crossed the Teviot immediately to the north of Hawick and then headed west, following its north bank. Within a mile or two, however, they would have deviated from the first path along another which ran south-west, through the broad valley of the Borthwick Water, eventually reaching the tiny settlement of Craik where a terrace of former Forestry Commission employees' houses now stands.

Along the way they would also have passed the habitations of Roberton and Hoscote, modern place names shown as already existing on the Roy Military Map but also in the *Atlas of Scotland* published a century earlier by the Amsterdam based printer Joan Blaeu.[11] The beautifully illustrated maps within this publication were based in turn upon the survey work carried out by the Scottish cleric Timothy Pont in the 1590s[12] and suggest that this route was already well-established by the middle ages.

Further evidence for the popularity of the route lay in a drove road which joined or crossed the footpath a mile or two before Craik and which may have continued beyond that settlement south-east towards Langholm or, just as likely, along the route that the Patersons were about to take into the valley of the Esk.[13] After passing Craik, however, the brothers would have started walking along a Roman road, the remains of which would have been still quite visible at this time, testifying to the antiquity of the route being followed. The road was part of what is thought to have been a network of Roman highways in Scotland, used during two relatively brief occupations of the country in the second and third centuries AD, respectively.

This particular highway is thought to have linked the fort at Torwood, near Lockerbie, to the south, with Newstead, near Melrose, to the north-east and possibly ran beyond that to the Forth.[14] The section on which the brothers would have walked ran from Craik in a straight line to the Roman fortlet at Raeburnfoot, near Eskdalemuir, going over Craik Cross Hill on the way where, as the name suggests, there is thought to have been a wayside cross for pilgrims using this route in the middle ages.[15] Despite the incredibly remote and rugged terrain through which the path passes today, in contemporary terms this was a major thoroughfare that appears to have continued in use for some 1600 years.

The road would have borne the brothers with relative ease to a ford of the White Esk just beyond the Roman fortlet. In fact, given the extent to which the modern site has been eroded by the river, its waters were probably already lapping against the banks of the fort when the brothers reached it. Once across the river they would have continued over moorland to cross the Black Esk at the appropriately named Sandyford. (Both rivers converge later in their journeys to form the Esk that runs through Langholm.) They would then have descended into the more heavily cultivated valley of the Dryfe Water and, much as the modern road does, turned south for Lockerbie, reaching it after a journey from Hawick of less than thirty-five miles or two comfortable days' walking.

Lockerbie at this time consisted of just a single row of cottages and two towers – strongholds of the Johnstone family – but was on the cusp of a period of fast growth. Already a regional market for cattle and sheep, the village was the subject of planned development which saw work begin on a new main street the following year and the completion of a new church and a second street, crossing the former, within another twenty years.[16] As a measure of their farsightedness, the Johnstones were granting unusually long leases on the properties: according to the Old Statistical Account, they "feued house steadings and tacks in 1730 for four score times 21 years." The development of a commercial awareness amongst local landowners, of which this is an early example, was an important facet of the development of the Scottish economy as the eighteenth century progressed.

Francis may have been anxious to press on without entering the village or he may have led Robert into Lockerbie to stock up on provisions before completing their journey as well as giving his brother his first glimpse of one of their two nearest settlements of any size. Either way, their ultimate destination was a cottage or possibly collection of cottages at Caldwell, on the west bank of the River Annan, some three miles north of Lochmaben, the other main settlement of the area. Their remaining route lay over a ford of the Water of Dryfe, just outside Lockerbie, and then a bridge over the Annan at a spot marked as 'Mills' on the Military Map and known as Millhousebridge today.

Caldwell
Francis, who was ten years Robert's senior, had by this time served his apprenticeship and was already earning his living as a stonemason. According to Robert Paterson junior, writing nearly a hundred years later,[17] Francis lived at Caldwell and worked in the nearby quarries on Corncockle Moor - there is a suggestion that he had by this time acquired the lease of his own quarry.[18]

The quarries, and the land around them, were in turn owned by the Jardine Family whose principal seat was at Jardine Hall, a mere stone's throw away on the east side of the river; in fact the Military map shows a path leading from the quarries to a river crossing point just to the north from where another path doubled back to the big house. The building of Jardine Hall, which had started in 1710, was one of the main reasons for the establishment of the local quarries on a commercial footing.

The site is still a working quarry today, though much expanded. It was noted in the early nineteenth century for the discovery of dinosaur prints in its rocks.* Sir William Jardine, the then baronet, was also a noted botanist/scientist of the period and later produced a book describing various finds made at Corncockle.[19]

---

* The discoveries were made by local quarry workers in 1813/14 but publicised by the Rev. Henry Duncan who wrote and lectured on them in the 1820s.

The Jardine family were long-established in the region. One Humphrey de Jardine is recorded as a witness to a land charter near Gretna as early as 1153 while the baronetcy, created by the Bruces, Lords of Annandale, was conferred on an Anglo-Norman called 'de Gardin' who fought and died at the battle of Dornock in 1333. In the fifteenth and sixteenth centuries, the family were one of the more powerful clans in the south-west of Scotland and forged strong alliances with the neighbouring Scotts and Johnstones as circumstances dictated. This was illustrated by the marriage in 1604 of Sir Alexander Jardine to Elizabeth Johnstone, daughter of Sir John Johnstone of Johnstone and his wife, Margaret Scott of Buccleuch.

The relevance of this is that the newlywed couple were responsible for the development of Spedlins Tower, the subsequent family base and predecessor to Jardine Hall, which still stands prominently on the west bank of the Annan. It is about half a mile north of Corncockle Moor and would have acted as a landmark for the Patersons as they approached home. The first baronet was not actually created until May 1672, during the reign of Charles II, although by Robert Paterson's time the family were well established financially through trading and land acquisition. The annual rental of the Spedlins Estate by 1755 was some £3000 sterling.[20]

As Francis was still in the early years of his career, it is unlikely that Robert would have learnt his trade under his brother even if, in all likelihood, they worked closely together. According to the estate records for this period,[21] one of the masons employed on the building of Jardine Hall was "John Forrest of Caldwell" and the assumption must be that it was to this man that Robert was apprenticed. An apprenticeship lasted for anything between five and twelve years but seven years was the average. During this time Robert's family would have been required to pay for his food, lodging and equipment in return for his training. Thereafter, as with his brother, he became a journeyman, ie. one who works for a day wage (after the French *journée*). Following further practical exams, once he had a body of experience and solid achievement behind him, the mason could aspire to becoming a master.

As for Francis Paterson, he appears to have made a home and career for himself in the area, eventually marrying Elizabeth Turnbull. He became a well-established mason, in demand for a number of locally significant building projects in later years. In 1757 the Commissioners of Supply contracted with him as the mason to rebuild the bridge over the Water of Milk at Holmhead, to the south of Lockerbie at a price of £107 16s.[22] Francis Paterson was also the mason commissioned to build the 'new' parish church of Applegarth, two miles south of Caldwell, in 1763. The Old Statistical Account of 1792 said of the resulting building that "It is large and well built and sufficient at present to contain the whole inhabitants of the parish."[23]

In the same year, Francis won the commission to rebuild the manse and associated offices for the parish church of Closeburn, in Nithsdale, within a couple of miles of the quarry that his brother would by this time have already acquired and vacated. But, of course, all this is in the future.

A Changing World
What did Robert experience on this journey and how should we imagine that he felt about it? Times were certainly changing and some signs of this would almost certainly have been evident along the way, giving the brothers something to talk about on their journey or after their arrival.

The cattle trade was expanding and bringing more local prosperity with it. This would already have been impacting on Paterson's family and their wellbeing but he might also have seen physical evidence along the route in terms of animal numbers, cattle drovers or local businesses – such as blacksmiths - being established to cater for them and even a cattle 'tryst' or two.

The population was also increasing, though marginally, with more people apparent in the settlements through which they passed as well as in the country generally. There would have been a greater demand for houses as a result, certainly evidenced by the increasing size and luxury of the houses of the rich and powerful, but villages were also growing in size and some were becoming towns. And, as we have seen, some of this was creating a demand for building stone, with implications for Robert's new career.

Whether Robert understood the potential of all is another matter. It is difficult to see into the mind of a thirteen year-old at any time, let alone of one living in the early eighteenth century. Times were harder, nothing could be taken for granted and maturity – in terms of a practical understanding of what had to be done to live - came more quickly. For people of Robert's background, who were the majority in Scotland at this time, expectations were low.

This is not to dismiss the potential for ambition in individuals but even where that existed it was exercised with a certain degree of pragmatism. Robert did not necessarily see the potential in what was new and different which might therefore have limited his excitement. Grounded in a proud history, strong local traditions and a strict religious code, he would have found it difficult, and would have had little encouragement, to see things other than as they were.

For the moment, we must therefore imagine Robert quite simply and straightforwardly as a young man wide-eyed at the sight of the new world that lay beyond the confines of Hawick, impressed by the knowledge and experience of his older brother, with whom he was probably spending more time than ever before, and excited, as well as nervous, at the prospect of starting his career. All of this would have been enough to compensate for the sadness he would have felt at leaving home for the first time and for any homesickness he might have felt in the coming days and weeks - it is unlikely that Robert would have returned home more than once or twice a year.

Notes

1   Haldane, ARB, *The Drove Roads of Scotland*, Edinburgh, 1971
2   Robertson J, *The public roads & bridges in Dumfriesshire 1650-1820*, Wigtown, 1993
3   *Ibid*
4   *The Two Drovers* features in *Chronicles of the Canongate* (Constable, 1896), Edinburgh University Library
5   Roy Military Survey of Scotland, 1747-1755, National Library of Scotland
6   Bain, J (ed.) *Calendar of documents relating to Scotland preserved in Her Majesty's Public Record Office*, 1887, quoted on RCAHMS website record for Branxholme Castle.
7   Description of the Parish of Langholm 1726, taken from *MacFarlane's Geographical Collections*, Scottish History Society, 1907.
8   Ibid. The Old Statistical Account for Dumfriesshire, Langholm Parish, 1793, also confirms that the tower, which dated from the early 16th century, had been demolished in 1725.
9   MacFarlane, op cit.
10 Ibid.
11 Blaeu Atlas of Scotland 1654, National Library of Scotland
12 Pont Maps Website, National Library of Scotland.
13 These routes are conjectured by Haldane, *op cit*. However, a modern footpath now runs cross country to Craik and is signposted as 'The old drove route from Hawick to Craik'.
14 Although hypothesised as such by a number of the Statistical Account parish records and other early survey documents, the existence of this Roman road network has only been confirmed through research, on the ground surveys and excavations since the 1940s. See, for example, Ian Richmond, *A New Roman Mountain-Road in Dumfriesshire and Roxburghshire* (1946) and Angus Graham, *The Roman Road to Raeburnfoot* (1948), Transactions of the Society of Antiquaries of Dumfries and Galloway (Transactions), vols.80 and 82, respectively.
15 RCAHMS website record for Craik Cross
16 Old Statistical Account for Dumfriesshire, Lockerbie Parish, 1792
17 Robert Paterson junior to Joseph Train, 20 September 1827, reprinted in Ramage, CT, *Drumlanrig Castle & the Douglases*, 1876. This letter forms the basis of Joseph Train's letter of 31 March 1829 to Sir Walter Scott which was mentioned in the last chapter. It is referred to again in later chapters.
18 Hewison, JK, *op cit*
19 Jardine, W, *Ichnology of Annandale: illustrations of footmarks impressed in the new red sandstone of Corncockle Muir*, Edinburgh, 1853.
20 Old Statistical Account for Dumfriesshire, Applegarth & Sibbaldie Parish, 1792
21 Family papers, Survey 3252, Jardine of Applegirth, National Archives of Scotland
22 Robertson, J, *The public roads and bridges..., op cit.*
23 OSA, Applegarth & Sibbaldie Parish, *op cit.*

CHAPTER FOUR

RED FREESTONE

The Quarrying and Building Tradition
The trade which Robert learned had not changed in its essentials since Roman times. Until the eighteenth century, rather than relying on professionally cut stone from a regional quarry, it was normal to find stone locally, either by pilfering from the ruined buildings of earlier generations or by quarrying whatever stone was available in nearby outcrops, whatever the quality. Roman and medieval quarries had been just surface pits, used until the more easily accessible resources ran out and it was time to find another convenient stone deposit. Stone was only brought from further afield if it was necessary for a particular purpose or desirable for the grandest buildings.

While Robert was learning his trade there was certainly no hint within his profession of the industrial processes which would be demanded by the proliferation of country houses, planned towns and villages and other developments to come within a generation in Dumfriesshire. The skills and practices involved in stone quarrying and stonemasonry in the region had nonetheless been perpetuated over the centuries through the demand created by a number of major cultural, architectural and other building projects; indeed as long as local residents had wanted to leave a permanent record of their existence and their activities.

It is evident in the crudely shaped boulders which form stone circles, such as the 'Seven Brethren' that Robert and his brother may have passed on the outskirts of Lockerbie, or the 'Loupin' Stanes' near their river crossing point in Eskdalemuir, both of which have been dated to the second millennium BC. It is also apparent in the Bronze Age cup-and-ring markings on rocks and boulders which abound in the region and it can be seen in the dressed stone blocks which were used to build the iron age forts which litter many local hills and cliff tops.

The Romans also had a great influence in the region, both on techniques for quarrying and dressing stone and in the monuments they left behind, of which advantageous use was made by subsequent builders. As Roman quarrying operations were confined mainly to outcrops and relatively shallow surface working, this has made it difficult to locate the sites of their quarries. However, remnants of Hadrian's Wall, to the south of our region, and a number of forts and camps north of it can be found in the later buildings which surround them. The now derelict church at Hoddomcross in Annandale, for example, is supposed to contain a stone or two from the ruins of the nearby Roman Camp of Birrens, including an altar which was inserted into the church porch.

The region also boasts a tradition of decorated stone crosses, a legacy of early Christian colonisers. Their presence is most obvious at Whithorn Priory, Wigtownshire, founded by St Ninian as early as the turn of fourth and fifth centuries. The influence of these - predominantly Irish - settlers is witnessed by numerous early churches, monasteries and burial grounds which spread from this centre throughout Galloway.

From the east, in the eighth to tenth centuries, came the Northumbrians whose Anglian culture and architectural style were similarly influential and widespread. Their inheritance can be seen in the exquisite Ruthwell cross, near Annan, and the broken, freestanding cross at Knockhill, Hoddom, in Annandale, as well as many other carved stones and crosses which are now housed in Dumfries Museum. According to local records, a stone cross, apparently hewn from the local rock by early Christians, stood near the quarry leased by Robert at Gatelawbridge until the end of the nineteenth century and an eroded Anglian stone cross still stands in a field near Thornhill, just a few miles away.

By the middle ages stone was being extensively used in the construction of the grander buildings of the region, particularly tower houses, castles and monasteries, built at the expense of monarchs and regional overlords. Tower houses were represented by nearby Spedlins but also Amisfield, Gilnockie and Bonshaw Towers, scattered to the south of the area in which Robert served his apprenticeship.

Of the castles, perhaps the best examples are: Lochmaben Castle, three miles south of Spedlins, built by Edward I; the magnificent Caerlaverock Castle, on the Solway coast, one of the most formidable and best preserved Scottish medieval castles and the home of the Maxwells until the Civil War; Morton Castle, in Nithsdale, only a mile north-west of Gatelawbridge, which dates back to the fourteenth century and which was formerly in the ownership of the Douglas family; and the equally splendid Drumlanrig Castle, of which more later.

The principal abbey ruins of the region, each a representative of the great medieval Cistercian abbeys of Scotland, are Lincluden, near Dumfries, Dundrennan Abbey, east of Kirkcudbright, and Sweetheart Abbey, south-west of Dumfries.

'New Red' Sandstone
The factor which all of these projects had in common was their proximity to a plentiful supply of good quality stone which was easily quarried and carved. The sandstone of Dumfriesshire was, and still is, much sought after for its fine grain and colour, which varies from the lightest pink to buff to a deep terracotta, as well as for the relative ease with which it can be cut. As James Richardson explained in *The medieval stone carver in Scotland*:

"If the stone easily answers to the mason's chisel and can be shaped and carved at the will of the hewer, that stone is then a freestone and, so far as Scotland is concerned, a sandstone."[1]

The sandstone originated about 250 million years ago, during what geologists refer to as the Permian period, a time when much of the area which is now northern Europe was nearer to the equator and had an arid, desert-like climate. During this time most of what later became Dumfriesshire was covered in sand dunes up to 250 metres deep and several miles wide. Over millions of years, and changes in climate, these sandy deposits were either washed away as sea levels rose once more or solidified, as happened in many parts of central Dumfriesshire, under the pressure of other rocks as the Earth's crust folded and cracked. The legacy is the deposits of 'New Red' or Permian sandstone which are found on or near the surface of many parts of Dumfriesshire and some parts of Galloway, shaped and eroded by the action of glaciers, rivers and general weathering in more recent geological times.

The geographical distribution of these deposits, or basins, is crucial to an understanding of the location of key periods in Robert Paterson's life and career because, by tradition, masons tended to live near the source of the stone with which they worked, even if the results of their work were subsequently transported many miles across the country. In this respect, in particular, Robert adhered closely to tradition, choosing the location of his home and work not by accident or on a whim but by the need to be close to the material he used. As we shall see, the distribution of sandstone across the region thus dictated where Paterson lived, worked and, ultimately, where he died.

To the north-east of Dumfries are two areas, known respectively by the towns on which they are centered as the Lochmaben Basin and the Moffat Basin.[2] The former is the larger area and is roughly rectangular in shape but tilted along a south-east/north-west axis. The town of Lochmaben lies just south of the centre of this deposit and Lockerbie is on the eastern fringe. Corncockle Moor, in Applegarth parish, where Robert learnt his trade, is at the very centre.

Although there were two main quarries at the heart of the moor, one of which is still worked today, there were several much smaller sites scattered about the periphery, leased to local men such as Francis Paterson. These were already marked as 'old quarries' on the First Edition Ordnance Survey map of the area in 1857, and appear to have been abandoned in favour of the commercial exploitation of the main sites as quarrying became a significant local industry.

By the middle of the nineteenth century the local stone was being transported across Scotland (it can be found in the Kelvin Hall in Glasgow) and even exported overseas. As noted in the previous chapter, Corncockle Moor is nonetheless most famous in archaeological circles for the discovery of fossilised dinosaur prints by quarryworkers at the beginning of the nineteenth century and for the contribution which this made to the early debates on evolution.[3]

Another, irregular shaped, deposit lies independent of these two to the north-west of Dumfries. It surrounds the village of Thornhill, which gives its name to the basin. The deposit is roughly four miles wide at its fattest and about twelve miles from north to south. From Barjarg Tower in the south-west, it stretches past Thornhill and then points north, like a finger, to the mouth of the Dalveen Pass which splits the Lowther Hills. To the east of Thornhill is the hamlet of Gatelawbridge to which Paterson and his family later moved and where he took a lease on a local sandstone quarry.

The largest is the Dumfries Basin, oval in shape and leaning diagonally south-east to north-west, from the Solway Firth up to Friars Carse, on the west bank of the River Nith. In parts of this area the sandstone bed has been estimated to be 1000m thick. The area incorporates the town of Dumfries and, two to three miles to the north-east, the village of Locharbriggs which has the largest sandstone quarry in the region.

Smaller quarries were scattered about the west of the region, and through Ayrshire, and would have been a source of stone for Paterson while on his wanderings through the middle and later parts of his life. Several quarries were also once worked to the south of Dumfries, in Caerlaverock parish, with easy access to the local port at Glencaple from where stone could be transported more efficiently by sea to other towns in the region, or across the Solway Firth to England. It was from the quarry at Bankend, in this area, that Paterson was apparently acquiring stone just prior to his death.

Paterson's Quarry
Gatelawbridge is a hamlet about eighteen miles north of Dumfries. It consists of a number of late Georgian or Victorian cottages and houses and two or three more modern bungalows astride a narrow country lane which zig-zags uphill from the nearby town of Thornhill. The older buildings include two rows of terraced – probably ex-farm labourers' – cottages and a converted barn, the old blacksmith's cottage and three much larger houses, of which one is the old poorhouse for Mid-Nithsdale, now converted into private houses.

Once a busy, thriving community, it is today a quiet and unassuming location, pleasant without being picturesque. The buildings betray little of the industry which gave rise to their construction or on which the hamlet was founded. With little or nothing to interest them, visitors usually pass through the area, following the lane as it bends once more, runs over the shaded Cample Water in the ravine below and continues uphill.

But Gatelawbridge, in common with many neglected hamlets or otherwise unremarkable settlements in Dumfriesshire, has a history. A clue to it can be found by walking down one of the two dirt tracks that diverge from between the old farm cottages, straying into the thick vegetation that borders them, past the signs marked 'Danger - No Entry', and then peering through the tall wire fence that stops pedestrians going any further, eventually to notice a line of stone cliffs in the distance. For those willing to ignore the signs the reason for the warning becomes apparent only ten metres beyond the fence.

Dropping away some twenty-five metres into milky blue water are the sheer walls of a former sandstone quarry, the scale of which takes a few seconds to become apparent. From this standpoint, the quarry must be twenty metres across and runs away to the right for perhaps sixty or seventy - it is not possible to get close enough to the edge to be sure.

Local people will tell you that this was the quarry which was worked by Robert Paterson, some 270 years ago. Although the map evidence suggests that this is unlikely,* it is one of a number of quarries in the area that date from a period of intensive activity between the mid-nineteenth century and the First World War and serves to illustrate the scale of the later workings into which Paterson's quarry would long since have been subsumed. Robert's place of work would have been much smaller and more shallow and difficult to imagine in the middle of the yawning hole below.

There are, indeed, several candidates for Paterson's quarry, in a variety of locations and sizes. The largest, still worked until the 1990s and now flooded and landscaped, is half a mile to the east, over the river and behind the adjacent hamlet of Newton. Another, a few hundred metres to the north of Newton, is completely overgrown. A third, the favoured site, is in Gatelawbridge and lies through the trees on the other side of the lane but is now used as a local council landfill site, filled with decades of domestic waste and inaccessible to the public.

The fact remains that it did exist somewhere in the depths of these later workings and fitted into the long tradition of excavating and carving stone in Dumfries and Galloway, already described, which subsequently contributed to the region's economic growth during the industrial revolution.

Commercial Quarrying
An early stimulus to the *commercial* quarrying of sandstone, not intended for one specific building project, was the need for stone walls which were gradually but increasingly being used for enclosures in the eighteenth century. Building stone

---

* The Ordnance Survey six inches to a mile First Edition map of 1861 shows the area as it was surveyed in 1856. The hamlet is called Gateley Bridge and there is just one quarry marked on the west bank of the river, to the north of the settlement. By 1898 the same series map shows a 'New Quarry' to the south, in the location of the currently fenced-off quarry.

was also required for planned villages and estates which were being established by landlords needing to attract a reservoir of labour for their newly improved agricultural estates: the example of Lockerbie has already been mentioned and Langholm, in Eskdale, was another such development, as was Kirkpatrick-Durham, a few miles away in Kirkcudbrightshire. So was nearby Thornhill, the development of which is described in Chapter Five. By the middle of the eighteenth century, many small quarries were in operation across the county, most of them seasonal, further encouraged in their output by the proliferation of a number of fine mansions and large country houses.

One of the earliest and grandest houses to have been built from the local sandstone was nearby Drumlanrig Castle. It was almost entirely rebuilt, between 1679 and 1697, for the third Earl – and subsequently the first Duke - of Queensberry using pink sandstone from quarries on his own estate – most notably the King's Quarry, north-east of Carronbridge. At its height, the project employed more than thirty stonemasons. Tinwald House in Annandale, erected between 1738-40 for Charles Erskine, the Lord Advocate, was built of brick but faced in red sandstone from the quarry of Locharbriggs, just north of Dumfries. At Kirkton, less than two miles to the west, Carnsalloch House was built between 1754-59 for Alexander Johnson, a native of Galloway who had made his money in London. Locharbriggs quarry is also on its doorstep.

According to the Statistical Account of Scottish parishes, by 1794 some 125 tons of sandstone annually were being exported from Cove Quarry in Kirkpatrick-Fleming, Annandale - recognised as the source of a particularly fine, 'white' sandstone - through the port of Annan to the south.[4] Similar quantities were being shipped out through Glencaple, on the Nith, as a result of quarrying in Caerlaverock parish. Much of the sandstone was in the form of dressed flagstones, being exported to form pavements in the expanding cities of Liverpool and Dublin. By the middle of the nineteenth century, there were some twenty-five commercial sandstone quarries in Dumfriesshire.

At the height of its production, in the late 1890s, the quarry at Gatelawbridge - together with the King's Quarry to the north - employed over a hundred people. Using the latest technology they produced some 400 tons of sandstone a week in excavations which descended to about thirty-five metres.[5] This was under the ownership of William Thomson and Sons who worked the quarry from 1868 until 1903. The layout of the village, whose population was sufficient to support a school, included cranes, tramways, dressing sheds, a blacksmith's shop for making and sharpening tools and pumps for water powered machinery and to drain water from the quarry.

The legacy of this development can be seen in two of the larger houses in the hamlet, mentioned earlier. They are, in fact, the former quarry manager's house and a quarry warehouse or loading shed, respectively. The two dirt tracks either side of the fenced-off quarry are also the beds of former railway lines: the scale of the operation allowed investment in a narrow gauge railway which transported stone from the quarry down to the main line, a mile away. From there the stone was carried away to be used in some of the larger Victorian buildings, not just of Dumfries and Galloway, but across the south of Scotland in Ayr, Glasgow and Edinburgh.

Through the Solway ports of Annan, Silloth and Maryport (the last two in Cumbria) as well as ports on the Clyde, the stone was also borne over the Atlantic, serving sometimes as ballast in ships' holds but also as part of direct orders for the construction of a number of prominent municipal, commercial and residential buildings in towns and cities such as Albany (in New York State), Boston and Montreal.[6]

The stonemason
These events were, of course, well in the future and beyond imagination as far as Robert Paterson was concerned, but they nonetheless provide a context for the development of the profession into which he entered.

In Scotland during the eighteenth and nineteenth centuries, sandstone was known as a 'freestone' - with 'red' or 'white' being added depending on the local shading. This was the name given to any stone which answered easily to the mason's chisel and could be shaped and carved without difficulty - hence the term 'freemason' which applied to one who cut and shaped freestone. A distinction was made between this and a 'rough mason' who usually worked at the quarry face. The latter worked with a mason's axe, exploiting the natural faults and brittleness of the rock to produce the blocks of raw material which could then be roughly shaped according to demand.

It is not clear in which field Robert Paterson specialised because it is apparent from his later career that he was adept in both, not unreasonable for someone who worked largely by himself. Paterson's outputs were, nonetheless, also rather more prosaic. To begin with at least, he appears to have produced sandstone for a variety of local uses, including stone for local buildings and roofs, but gradually his output became geared to one particular market which was also expanding in the eighteenth century - the demand for gravestones.

The technology employed by Paterson in quarrying and shaping his stones would also have been fairly limited. In fact, as we have seen, it owed more to the Romans than to the fast approaching industrial revolution. As James Richardson noted, "The fragments of a pilaster, hewn by a mason for a building within the Roman fort at Inveresk, Midlothian, when compared with work produced by a Scottish mason, bear such a resemblance to the latter that without the knowledge that they were found associated with a Roman building, they might easily have been deemed fragments of a seventeenth century gravestone."[7]

Quarrying of outcrops of softer stone such as sandstone was by 'guttering'. Long, deep channels were hewn out of the surface of the rock with special picks which divided the rock into large blocks. These were then detached from the bed using long bars and then cut down to size employing a similar technique on each block. By Paterson's time, it is possible that long, two-handled saws were used to cut smaller blocks to shape.

The stones were then dressed, that is cut to shape (for example as gravestones, or stones for buildings or walls), at the quarry side to make them easier to transport and to save time later. The blocks could be quite large, weighing several tons or more, and had to be brought under the mason's hammer and squared with a tool called a 'kivel' which in itself could weigh up to twenty pounds. All of which would have been second nature to an experienced mason. As Kenneth Hudson comments on the Portland stone quarrying tradition in Dorset at this period:

> "The quarrymen are so accustomed to the work that they can guide the tool with the utmost precision and, by keeping time with each other, make every stroke effective."[8]

Thus apprenticed and with the benefit of a few additional years of work as a journeyman, perhaps contracted to John Forrest or in helping his brother with his developing career, by the early 1740s Robert was ready to set out on his own.

Notes

1   Richardson, James, *The medieval stone carver in Scotland*, Edinburgh, 1948.
2   *British Regional Geology: the South of Scotland* (NERC, 1971) & *A Practical Geography of Dumfriesshire*, J Murray, Dumfries, 1921.
3   In 1827, for example, the Reverend Henry Duncan wrote and gave a lecture on 'An account of the tracks and footmarks of animals found impressed in sandstone in the quarry of Corncockle Muir in Dumfriesshire'. The prints themselves had been discovered in 1813/14. Sir William Jardine, the then baronet, was also a noted botanist/scientist of the time and produced a volume of the finds at Corncockle entitled *Ichnology of Annandale: illustrations of footmarks impressed in the new red sandstone of Corncockle Muir* (Edinburgh 1853).
4   Statistical Account of Scotland 1791-99, Vol.iv, Dumfriesshire.
5   *Dumfries & Galloway Standard*, 31 October 1896.
6   Hawkins, James Irving, *The Sandstone Heritage of Dumfriesshire*, 2001.
7   Richardson, J, *op cit*
8   Hudson, Kenneth, *The Fashionable Stone*, Adams & Dart, 1971.

CHAPTER FIVE

COURTSHIP, MARRIAGE AND HOME

Stepping Out
According to Paterson's son, Robert junior, following his apprenticeship his father served "for some considerable time afterwards" as a journeyman working with his brother Francis. Eventually, however, he came "to the time of life that was proper to choose some way of doing for himself".[1] In this endeavour he appears to have had some assistance from his future wife.

Elizabeth Gray was the daughter of Robert Gray, the gardener at Jardine Hall which, as Robert junior noted, was "within loud speaking" of Caldwell, the hamlet in which Paterson lived with his brother. Born in 1726, Elizabeth was ten years younger than Robert who, apprenticed to one of the masons who had built the Hall, would have had good reason to visit the property on a regular basis. He would therefore have watched her grow up until, at the age of fourteen, she went to work in the kitchens of Closeburn House, in Nithsdale, about twenty miles to the west: her son recorded her working there by the winter of 1740 which, as described in Chapter Two, was one of a number of hard winters that afflicted the eighteenth century. Robert junior recorded it as being "still memorable for frost".[2]

Closeburn formed part of the estate of Sir Thomas Kirkpatrick whose family had been resident in Dumfriesshire since Norman times. His ancestors dated back in an almost unbroken line to 1190 when records refer to one Ivo de Kirkpatrick and his son, also Ivo, who died in 1232.[3] They appear to have taken their name from the existence of a local chapel dedicated to Saint Patrick, the patron saint of Ireland whose birthplace is supposed to have been in Cumbria.

Another ancestor, Roger Kirkpatrick, served with Robert the Bruce in the Anglo-Scottish wars of the early fourteenth century. He was by the future king's side in March 1306 when the latter stabbed John de Comines, Lord of Badenoch, known as the 'Red Comyn' and a fellow claimant to the Scottish throne, before the altar of Greyfriars Church in Dumfries. Kirkpatrick, upon hearing his companion's confession, showed remarkable *sang froid* by returning to the scene of the crime to make sure, as the popular attribution goes, that Comyn was dead. The family crest and motto, "I mak siccar" (I will make sure), is carved into the east gable of the church ruins in Closeburn churchyard.

In October 1727 Sir Thomas, the third Baronet of Closeburn, married Susan Grierson whose father, James Grierson of Capenoch, had died earlier in the year, leaving her to inherit. The marriage thus saw the merger of their properties producing an estate which stretched for some ten or twelve miles along both banks of the Nith, from Holywood, just north of Dumfries at the southern end of the valley, to the site of the former medieval village of Dalgarnock, in mid-Nithsdale, by this time long abandoned.

The Kirkpatricks were therefore major landowners whose property boundaries ran contiguously along their northern and eastern edges with those of the mighty Douglas family, from whom Paterson was soon to lease his quarry. Charles Douglas, the then third Duke of Queensberry, was a minister in George II's government and his father, who had been instrumental in negotiations over the Union in 1707, served for two years as Secretary of State for Scotland under Queen Anne.

The ambitions of both families were reflected in the building of grand local houses towards the end of the seventeenth century: the Douglases through the development of Drumlanrig Castle, completed in 1697 on the site of a former tower house; and the Kirkpatricks through Closeburn House, built in part from the stones of a nearby tower house of the fourteenth century. The Douglases were also building what was to become the ducal town of Thornhill, just across the Cample Burn which divided the two estates. It was an amalgamation of the existing hamlet of Thornhill and the new, planned development of New Dalgarnock immediately to the north-east.

In addition, the estate records for Drumlanrig for 1740-45 show contributions to the construction of a new manse for the minister of Penpont parish and, significantly for our story, towards the building of a new church at Closeburn in 1741. (The church was not on Queensberry land but was in the same presbytery as Penpont and the payment could have been negotiated by Sir Thomas Kirkpatrick as the two families were very close.) During the same period there was also considerable expenditure on the grounds of the estate itself, for example in 1742 for the creation of new roads in the park surrounding the castle.[4]

The quarrying activity resulting from all these developments created a demand for stonemasons as well as a range of other tradesmen and ancillary services. This fitted into a pattern of emerging industry and associated development as the eighteenth century progressed. Scottish landowners competed to attract and retain skilled workers for the industries emerging out of the natural resources on their doorstep, as well as tenants for the towns and villages they were creating to house the existing agricultural population and establish markets for their produce.

In similar fashion to the development of Lockerbie on the back of the livestock trade, the Queensberry Estate sought to attract tradesmen to move to Thornhill by advertising inducements such as free materials for their trade and even accommodation if they were willing to build their own houses. The Board of

Trustees for Fisheries, Manufactures and Improvements had been established as early as 1727 to assist landowners nationwide in these and similar endeavours, focusing mainly on the weaving and fishing industries. An advert was printed by the Board in Edinburgh a few years after Paterson's time in Nithsdale which nonetheless exemplified the approach being taken in the area and the obvious opportunity for a good stonemason to exploit:

> "The Duke of Queensberry ... advertises that all weavers and nailers, from whatever part they come, shall have ground sufficient for a house and garden rent-free for 19 years with liberty of raising stone in his Grace's quarries and some wood for building, the houses to be situated as the tradesmen shall incline... in the village of Thornhill... the houses to be built according to plans in the possession of his Grace's factor at Drumlanrig of stone and lime, or at least with stone and mortar, rough cast with lime."[5]

By the early 1740s, in his mid-twenties, Robert Paterson would not have been unaware of the possibilities for the development of his career in and around Thornhill. But how tempting they might have been compared with the plentiful work on his doorstep is unclear. At least two factors would have been crucial in swaying his judgement. The first was very likely the gentle pressure from his brother, in his mid-thirties and already married, to make space for his new family. The second was the coming of age of Elizabeth who would have turned sixteen in 1742 and entered at least her third year of service with the Kirkpatricks.

The precise sequence of events leading to Robert and Elizabeth's marriage and move to Morton Parish, in which Thornhill was situated, is unknown. However, their son, Robert junior, said that his mother, through her connections with the Kirkpatrick family, was instrumental in acquiring a lease from the Queensberry Estate on the quarry at what was then Gateley, or Gateley Brig, and is now Gatelawbridge.

A romantic interpretation of their story leans towards Elizabeth 'stepping out' with Robert on her occasional visits home and planting the notion in Robert's head of how pleasant life might be with his own business – and family - in Nithsdale. Once she had some firm indication from Robert that their futures were inextricably linked, Elizabeth might then have broached the subject with her existing employers, or at least the factor (land agent) for the Kirkpatrick estate. As we shall see in the next chapter, the Kirkpatricks were famously paternalistic towards their employees and tenants so the ability of a 'lowly' kitchen maid to enquire of opportunities for her fiancé, and for that enquiry to be received favourably, cannot be ruled out.

In a more realistic age, however, it is more likely that Robert only popped the question after securing a lease on the quarry and setting himself up in business. This could still have been with Elizabeth's help, even if she only made him aware of the opportunity, perhaps using her father as an intermediary through his position with the Jardine family.

Local tradition holds that Robert was involved in the construction of Closeburn Church which, as we have seen, was already underway in 1741.[6] In particular, Paterson is supposed to have inscribed the construction date above the chancel arch of the church. Though unsubstantiated, the story has the germ of truth because the stone for the church would have come from quarries at Newton, less than three miles north of the church site and just across the river from Gateley.

It is not unreasonable that a project of this size would have required the employment of skilled workers, including stonemasons, from outside the parish and that Robert might have been contracted accordingly. As already mentioned, Francis Paterson himself benefited from the letting of a later contract to rebuild the manse and associated offices at Closeburn, although his regional reputation had by that stage been well established. While working on the construction of the church as a journeyman stonemason, Robert could therefore have spotted the opportunity to take a lease on the quarry at Gateley and then put wheels in motion through his contact within the Kirkpatrick family who, after all, lived within 300 yards of the church and were its patrons.

Whatever the truth of the matter, it is almost certain that Robert was installed at Gateley within a year or so of the completion of the church at Closeburn, towards the end of 1742 or the beginning of 1743. Based on the date of birth of their first child, this would have given Robert the time to build a home for himself nearby and to establish his customers before he and Elizabeth were married.

A New Home
The location of the Patersons' home cannot be confirmed with any precision – as described in Chapter Four, building works associated with the Thomson family quarries in the later nineteenth century probably obliterated the signs of earlier developments. However, writing over eighty years later, Robert Paterson junior remembered that his father "built a substantial and comfortable house for himself and his family, with ground that kept one horse and one cow, at a moderate rent... in Morton parish",[7] that is to say on the west bank of the Cample Burn which divides Morton from Closeburn parish.

Robert junior added that his father took a lease of Gateleybridge (now Gatelawbridge) quarry which, as already described, is also on the west bank. Parish birth records (see later) also record the Patersons as living in 'Gatelabrig'. Newton, the nearest existing settlement, was only a matter of a few hundred yards from the quarry, but over the river in Closeburn parish. It seems reasonable that Robert would want to build his home on a separate site near his place of work and not have to cross what can be a fast-flowing stream at least twice a day to reach it.*

It is likely that the cottage that Robert built, using stone from his own quarry, would have been similar to that of his parents, ie. a 'but and ben' of neighbouring rooms, probably with an extension for the animals. Given his ready access to building materials, however, the dimensions of the property may have been more generous than his parents enjoyed. It would also have been thatched, as evidence suggests was the convention for the majority of houses in the parish.[8]

The wedding probably took place towards the end of 1743, most likely in Applegarth and Sibbaldie parish, in the medieval church that Francis would later win the commission to rebuild, although no records have survived to confirm the marriage date or location. Elizabeth would by then have quit her position at Closeburn Hall, leaving behind a salary of around thirteen or fourteen shillings a year, plus shoes and an apron, and gained instead a dowry from her father. Robert would have had savings from at least five years of paid employment.

Following the wedding, the newly married couple would have followed a route of about twenty miles to their first home, all on foot but probably with a pony to carry a few possessions, including recently acquired wedding gifts. As the crow flies, the terrain between the parishes of Applegarth and Morton was barren hill country, criss-crossed with rivers and streams and largely devoid of tracks or paths of any description. Even today, roads through the area, which is heavily forested, are narrow, winding and used only by local traffic. Instead, the traveller had to circumvent the area to the south, following a route which linked a number of historic settlements, together with their churches and tower houses.

From Jardine Hall they would have walked south to Lochmaben and then followed roads in a broad arc west then north-west. The route linked the settlements of Tinwald, clustered around its seventeenth century church, Amisfield, where the sixteenth century tower house of the Charteris family would have provided a landmark, and Dalswinton Old House and Tower, then in the hands of the Maxwell family, before descending into the Nith Valley. From here it headed north again, joining the old Dumfries to Sanquhar road at Auldgirth, after which it was a short distance to Closeburn and, for Elizabeth at least, familiar territory.

To reach Gateley from Closeburn the couple would have had the choice of following the Cample Burn north-east to the hamlet of Newtown (now Newton),

---

* The Rev Peter Rae (1671-1748), minister of Kirkconnel parish, further up the valley, recorded in his unfinished 'A Natural and Genealogical History of the Shire of Dumfries' that the Cample could be easily crossed here, but only with the help of a single stone thrown across the narrow ravine.

on the east bank of the stream, and crossing it at this point; or continuing north to cross the Cample over a stone bridge at Templand and then reaching their new home on established parish paths, taking stock of the burgeoning villages of Thornhill and New Dalgarnock *en route*. Given the time of year, with the possibility of the Cample being in spate and the need to stock up on provisions, the latter route would have been preferable.

Morton

The parish in which the couple lived has remained largely unchanged in its dimensions to this day. It covers an area of about thirteen square miles, enclosed, as we have seen, by the Cample Burn to the east and south and the River Nith to the west, beyond Thornhill. To the north, the Lowther Hills rise suddenly in a series of whaleback folds in the landscape, marking the boundary of the Southern Upland Fault from which the broad, flat agricultural lands of the Nith Valley run away to the south.

The name of the parish was apparently derived from Norse words which translated as a "great fort" or "fort on the moor", possibly a reference to an early predecessor of Morton Castle, a late fourteenth century structure, the substantial ruins of which stand only two miles to the north of Gatelawbridge. One of a number of castles which were built during the middle ages to guard entrances to the steep-sided mountain passes beyond, Morton belonged to a branch of the Douglas family which had been in residence in the area since the mid-fourteenth century. According to baptism records for the parish the castle was still in occupation when Robert and Elizabeth moved to the area[9], albeit only by tenants.

The principal residence of the Douglases by the 1740s was Drumlanrig Castle, just outside the western boundary of the parish but viewable from any high point within it. Indeed, the Douglases owned nearly all the land within the parish, and attended mass in their own specially commissioned church at Durisdeer, another couple of miles north of Morton Castle, where family members were buried in the vaults beneath. They were surmounted by a marble *baldacchino,* or canopy, modelled on that of St Peter's, in Rome.

In an era when state or even local government intervention was minimal, the involvement of the ducal estate in the working lives of local residents was significant, whether for good or ill. Those who could afford it paid a standard rent of around five shillings a year to the estate,[10] plus *teinds* or taxes on relevant farm produce, but those who couldn't might expect to have their rents discharged, at least temporarily, and to pay them in kind through work on the estate or through other services and materials rendered, for example by helping to build or repair roads, mend fences and walls, weed fields and ditches or clear woods for fuel, and so on. Those in dire straits might also have received financial support out of a fund established by the estate for payments to individual "poor persons" in Morton and Durisdeer. In 1744 some £10 14s 9d was disbursed to deserving residents across the estate for this purpose.[11]

The estate also employed people directly on larger schemes of work of economic importance to the area. In 1746 the accounts record a sum of £5 18s towards "... sundry workmen and quarryers (sic) in account of their day's wages employed the years 1744 and 1745, in quarrying stones for building the Miln Dam and for heightening the walls of the Inn and taking down the old slate, wheeling out the rubbish, etc."[12]

However, this activity needs to be viewed in the context of a parish – indeed a region – that was very sparsely populated, even by contemporary standards. The Old Statistical Account estimated only 435 residents for the parish as a whole in 1755, ten years after the Patersons first moved in, of whom about half would have lived in Thornhill and perhaps another sixty in Carronhill (now Carronbridge) leaving just pockets of inhabitants scattered about the countryside.[13] Neighbours would have been distinguished not by their surnames, which were commonplace, but specifically by the places in which they lived, for example John Kerr of Shiel, Thomas Harkness of Mitchellslacks or John Grierson in Gaitsyd, to quote local gravestones.

Thornhill was then, as now, the largest settlement in the parish. It was founded during Charles I's reign, in 1639, as New Dalgano, a Burgh of Regality, though in reality it had no residents until 1664 when the centre of the ducal village of the Queensberry estate was formally established a few hundred yards south of its present centre. A market cross was erected and an inn built by 1714 as the village became a staging post *en route* from Dumfries to Glasgow and Kilmarnock. But no road of any description, or even the formal layout of the present town, were laid until much later in the eighteenth century.[14]

This low density of population, basic infrastructure and the subsistence nature of the agricultural economy were replicated across most of the Queensberry Estate at the time, indeed across much of south-west Scotland. It meant that the income that could be raised by the landlord from tenant rents, taxes on agricultural and industrial produce or other payments to the family for the use of their land was severely restricted.

Attempts were already being made by estates like Drumlanrig, and others in the bordering counties of Ayrshire and Lanarkshire, to put their arrangements on a more commercial footing. This involved, for example, the creation of single (rather than shared) tenancies to encourage farmers to be more independent and to sell their surpluses to market, rather than consuming them or giving them to the landlord as rent 'in kind', as we saw was still happening in Hawick earlier in the century. Tenants were also being granted longer leases (usually nineteen years) to give them the confidence to plan ahead and invest the proceeds of their sales. However, the results of these endeavours would not bear fruit for years to come.[15]

The Drumlanrig Estate accounts (which covered Morton, Durisdeer and part of the neighbouring Penpont parish) for 1743/44 record that just over £343 annually were raised in "rent, teinds and feus", an amount quickly eaten up by payments towards ministers' stipends, schoolmasters' salaries, payments towards poor relief and rents foregone, etc. which in the same year amounted to a little over £253.[16] The latter figure covered a slightly wider area which included the family's parish responsibilities in Sanquhar and in smaller landholdings along the Solway Firth, but the pattern was clear.

The income which the Duke derived in total from his estates across the south of Scotland added up to thousands of pounds and was huge by contemporary standards. However, the situation described above, compared to the wealth which he could see being created among his counterparts in England, accounted for the measures which he and landowners like him were beginning to take to encourage new industry to their own land and immigration to towns and villages.

Church and School
The church which Robert and Elizabeth attended was located in the centre of the parish, only a mile north-west of their home, a comparatively short Sunday stroll away. The site, on which a medieval church previously stood, dates from the twelfth century when the monks of Kelso, in the Scottish Borders, were granted the land. It became part of the Queensberry Estate in 1629 after which a new church must have been built because, according to the Presbytery Session records, the existing church was substantial enough to boast a bell tower of at least twenty feet in height in 1737 when a new bell was commissioned to hang in it, at a cost of £7 9s 6d, together with a rope of six fathoms in length.[17]

The minister at the time, and during most of the Patersons' time in the parish, was one Archibald Little. The Drumlanrig Estate accounts record annual payments during the 1740s of *teind* for the minister of £21 18s 4d[18]: a seemingly large sum for a year but one which it appears was intended to cover all the church's costs, including maintenance and fuel for heating plus distributions to the poor as well as the minister's salary. It was meant as a substitute for the monies that were normally paid directly by tenants but, as we saw in Hawick, frequently were not.

In similar fashion to Hawick, the church elders were also more than willing to intrude into the private affairs of parishioners and to castigate them when they fell short of the expected standards of the day. A typical entry in the presbytery session records for Penpont, which included Morton parish, was the one for 6

March 1751 which concerned the "scandal of fornication" between Robert Dalyell and Catherine Lorimer from Dabtoun (now Dabton, a private house within the parish) wherein she apparently bore his child after, she claimed, being dragged into Dalyell's mother's barn. The case had been referred to the kirk session for consideration and reproof as appropriate and progress was reviewed several times over the following year, with several witnesses from Morton parish brought forward and their testimonial recounted, before Dalyell admitted to the crime.[19]

The elders of Morton Kirk Session itself had a particularly direct approach to parishioners whom they suspected of "antinuptial fornication", typified by the following exchange involving Sarah Hunter in February 1759:

"Interrogated: if with child. Ans/d: she was
2nd: who was the father of her child. Ans/d: Alexander Kennedy in Kirkland who was her fellow servant
3rd: when was the guilt committed. Ans/d: about Whitsunday
4th: where was the guilt committed. Ans/d: in the fields."

Having confessed to their sin, the couple were ordered to appear publicly before the Congregation and to be "rebuked for their sin and scandal."[20]

Not very much is known about the minister himself but it would appear that he was popular with his parishioners. An entry in the presbytery records for 1 March 1759 includes a reference to a petition which had been raised against his "transportation" to Kirkpatrick-Irongray, ie. he was being poached by another parish, a not unusual occurrence at this period, as we also saw in Hawick. The petition, which was ultimately unsuccessful, was signed by six elders, one heritor and forty-four heads of families. (Robert Paterson is not among them, being absent from the parish by this date.) The transportation went ahead in April and in May the presbytery wrote to the Duke of Queensberry to advise him of the vacancy, a significant development of which more in the next chapter.

The church was rebuilt in 1781, long after the Patersons had left, but even by this date its location was proving inconvenient for parish residents, most of whom lived at least two miles down the hill in Thornhill. By 1839 it had been abandoned in favour of a new and much larger building in the town itself and was in ruins by 1898 when, according to James King Hewison, it was "wasted to the bell-gable".[21] Today only the ivy-clad north gable still survives, forming an atmospheric gateway in the middle of the churchyard, surrounded by gravestones of which several are likely to have been cut by Robert Paterson himself.

According to the baptism records for Morton Parish, Robert and Elizabeth had at least six children. The first to arrive was Margaret, born in October 1744. There followed: John, born in August 1747; Walter, born in August 1749; Francis, born in

May 1752; Janet, born in December 1753; and, finally, Robert (the Robert junior who is the principal primary source for Paterson's life), born in December 1756.

None of Paterson's other biographers refer to Francis, obviously named after the brother with whom Robert had been so close. Hewison (1898) only says that Robert and Elizabeth had "at least" three sons but he names them as John, Walter and Robert. Ramage (1876) says that Robert had five children and names them as John, Walter, Robert, Margaret and Janet. The inference is that Francis died in infancy and certainly before the family moved away from Gatelawbridge. There is no parish record of a death by that name but deaths were less frequently recorded in Scottish parishes, especially that of a child.

It is also curious that neither of the girls were named after their mother, although Robert junior, named after his father, was the last child. Margaret was named after Robert's mother while Walter was named after his father. It is not clear after whom Janet was named but it could have been Elizabeth's mother.

According to the Old Statistical Account, the first parish school was in a thatched cottage to the side of the church, built — or at least refurbished - in 1731 with the help of an endowment left by John McCaig of nearby Drumcork.[22] The kirk session minutes record a payment of £8 for repairs to the building. By the time the Paterson children were old enough to attend the teacher was Andrew Greggan, recorded in the Presbytery minutes as having been appointed "legal schoolmaster" in March 1745.[23] He was from Kirkbean, near the coast just south of Dumfries, and supplied a "certificate" from heritors of that parish attesting to his qualifications. According to the Presbytery records, a committee of the heritors of Morton parish had examined him and reported that they found him "qualified to teach Latine, English, Writing and Arithmitick (sic)".

The estate accounts later recorded the payment of Greggan's salary which, for the year from 13 February 1745 to 1746 amounted to £2 15s 6d.[24] In 1791 the Statistical Account recorded that this had only climbed to "100 merks Scotch (about £5)... with a house, a cow's grass, 3 roods of croft land and very small wages from the scholars"[25] and complained that it was "a trifling emolument", insufficient to attract properly qualified teachers. Despite this, and quite remarkably, Andrew Greggan was still in post at this time. According to Hewison he only retired in 1794, when the school was moved to Thornhill.[26]

The Quarrying Business

Robert Paterson's quarrying business appears initially to have thrived. In the early years at least, he profited from work for a wide range of building purposes and not just the gravestones which later marked him out. Robert junior said that his father worked as a "builder and hewer" on the Duke of Queensberry's estate, also finding employment with Sir Thomas Kirkpatrick. When Closeburn House burnt down in August 1748, destroying in the process the family papers, portraits and plate, it was not rebuilt: instead the family moved back into the old tower house (which a branch of the family still occupies to this day) and ordered sandstone slabs from Gatelawbridge quarry for a new roof.[27]

In his unfinished history of Dumfriesshire, written just before his death in 1748, the minister of nearby Kirkconnel parish, Peter Rae, commented of Morton parish that "There are several good free stone quarrys (sic) in the paroch, whereof Gatela Bridge is esteemed the best",[28] suggesting that Robert had indeed built up the reputation of his business by then.

Altogether, Robert junior commented, the demand which had been created allowed his father to employ "a number of men occasionally at least".[29] One of these employees appears to have been a Highland boy named Sandy Rae whom Paterson apprenticed in stonecutting. According to Robert junior, his father took the boy, who was an itinerant beggar *cum* jobseeker in the parish, under his wing when he began his travels into Galloway and frequently left him to finish pieces of work while he returned home. Ramage, in his history of Drumlanrig and the local area, commented in 1876 that this may account for the poor spelling on some of Paterson's headstones.[30]

Inevitably, however, much of Paterson's order book was comprised of gravestones: not just to mark the burial spots of the recently dead, but also to commemorate members of previous generations, including the Covenanting martyrs of the seventeenth century. The practice of entombment within the church had been banned after the Scottish Reformation of 1560. This led to a greater number of burials outside and to the proliferation of monuments in graveyards where previously there were very few. Up until that time, churchyards had been used as public open spaces for markets, fairs, military drills and the like. The erection of monuments in these spaces gradually encroached on these practices.

Those who could afford it got around the ban on burials within churches by having enclosures, known as 'aisles', built onto churches. The Kirkpatricks had joined an aisle onto Closeburn Church within a year of the latter's completion. Much later, the Victorians developed a fashion for developing burial enclosures out of the ruins of old churches.

Those less well off initially marked graves with simple foot or headstones, wooden crosses or not at all. However, as wealth in the country increased, a fashion for larger, formal gravestones gained momentum and the incorporation of lettering and carvings became steadily more customised and diverse. Funeral monuments ranged from the older style of slabs or 'trughs', which overlaid the grave completely; to table slabs raised horizontally two feet or so over the grave on four or more decorated plinths (with the sides often filled in, like sarcophagi); to the increasingly popular standing stones erected at the head of the grave.

By the mid-eighteenth century individually carved headstones proliferated with a huge range of emblems of mortality and immortality (skull and crossbones, hourglasses, the figure of Death with his scythe, angels, and so on), family figures and coats of arms and even trade markings, depending on the profession of the dead person.

Robert supplied the stone for these monuments, carved them to shape, transported them to the gravesides and chiselled the inscriptions to order. In his *Chiselprints of Mortality*,[31] Hewison discussed Paterson's style of stonecutting and engraving based on the stones in Nithsdale churchyards which were contemporary with his presence in the area. On the reverse of upright stones, which were usually about four feet high, "he carved winged angel heads, skulls, cross-bones, coffins, and the implements of trade, which were not common before". His style was to use the 'cursive' lettering (joined up writing) and, within the text, to repeat common phrases such as "Memento Mori" – although this could just as likely have been local customer preference, dictated by fashion. Around the slabs, sometimes sitting on six or eight carved supports, he inscribed "neat geometric forms and various patterns of leaves".

In many cases, of course, the deceased were buried beneath pre-existing, family headstones where Paterson was simply commissioned to add fresh inscriptions or re-cut earlier ones. Here it was important to understand the fashions of former generations. In the sixteenth and seventeenth centuries lettering on gravestones was in Latin or Latin and the Scottish vernacular, and was carved in Roman capitals, raised in high relief (excised), often with spaces, dots or lozenges between each word. Before the early seventeenth century, most lettering was also carved around the edge of the slab but, after a time, it progressed horizontally across the face of the stone. Letters and words were often run together to save space - bindings of the uprights of letters, as in 'THE' or 'LL', were an ancient device known as 'ligatures'.

These practices had largely died out by the beginning of the eighteenth century, by which time letters were more often incised. Paterson only used the old style of lettering when re-cutting older stones: "when left to his own devices", Hewison concluded, "he uniformly used the cursive character incised, avoided the excised, and retained the old, incised Roman lettering for martyrs' monuments only."

The Legacy
Work on the so-called martyrs' monuments was nonetheless an increasing part of Robert's business. The United Societies, which represented the Covenanting movement, had since the beginning of the eighteenth century begun to identify, index and mark the graves of their martyrs. This was fuelling demand, especially in the south-west of Scotland, for good stonemasons to produce tombs and inscriptions for loved ones. In addition to this social opportunity there was the

practical advantage that Paterson enjoyed in having ready access to sandstone which was the material used for the majority of memorials. As well as local orders, therefore, Paterson seems increasingly to have cultivated and met demand further afield, in areas to the west of Thornhill.

Robert junior's view was that his father saw the commercial opportunities inherent in carving out sandstone headstones and carrying them into Galloway, or other parts of the south-west of Scotland, where the materials were less readily available, and that this alone accounted for his increasing proclivity to travel and be away from home. But whether this was his principal motivation or whether Robert senior was by this point in his life more influenced by a desire to commemorate the Covenanters is a theme that needs further exploration.

Notes

1   Paterson, R, letter to Robert Train dated 20 September 1827, quoted by Ramage in *Drumlanrig Castle and the Douglases*, 1876, *op cit.*
2   ibid
3   The family background is described in *The Kirkpatricks at Capenoch, 1727-1846*, John Gladstone, Transactions of the Dumfries and Galloway Antiquarian Society III/15/85.
4   *A Drumlanrig Castle Estate Book 1740-45*, Transactions III Vol.18, p.85
5   National Library of Scotland, Queensberry Estate Accounts. The advert, dated 1763, is pasted on the back of a slim volume containing scraps of accounts for Drumlanrig Castle and the estate generally, apparently collected together for a private sale in 1903.
6   Watson RMF, *Closeburn Parish*, 1901
7   Paterson, R, *op cit*
8   OSA, Morton Parish, Dumfriesshire, 1793. The account says that, even as late as 1791, the majority of houses in the parish were thatched.
9   Hewison, JK, *Dalgarnoc*, 1936. Births were recorded by residents living in the castle grounds in 1746.
10 OSA, Morton parish, *op cit*. The account records the standard rent being 5s 4d by 1779.
11 Queensberry & Drumlanrig Estate Accounts 1736-47 (Hornel Library, Kirkcudbright)
12 ibid
13 OSA, Morton parish, *op cit*
14 ibid
15 Devine, TM, *The Transformation of Rural Scotland*
16 Estate Accounts 1736-47, *op cit*
17 Penpont Presbytery records for 1737-45, including records for Morton Parish, NLS CH2/298/4.
18 Estate Accounts 1736-47, *op cit*
19 Penpont Presbytery Records, *op cit*
20 Morton Kirk Session Records 1714-1810
21 Hewison, J K, *Chiselprints of Mortality*, *op cit.*
22 OSA, Morton parish, *op cit.*
23 Presbytery records, *op cit.*
24 Estate Accounts 1736-47, *op cit.*
25 OSA, Morton parish, *op cit.*
26 Hewison, JK, *op cit.*
27 Gladstone, J, *The Kirkpatricks at Capenoch, 1727-1846,* Transactions III/15/85.
28 Rae, Rev P, 'A Natural and Genealogical History of the Shire of Dumfries', unfinished 1748.
29 Paterson, R, *op cit*
30 Ramage, CT, *Drumlanrig Castle and the Douglases*, *op cit.*
31 Hewison, JK, *op cit*

Sir Walter Scott, Bust of 1820 by
Sir Francis Chantrey in Abbotsford House

Engraving of 'Old Mortality' from
Scott's Worthies, WS Crockett

A plaque erected to the memory of Joseph Train in Newton Stewart Town Hall and
(detail) his carved image

Exterior of Haggisha' c.1908, the gentleman
at the door was the tenant at the time

St Mary's Church and churchyard,
Hawick

The registration of Paterson's baptism
in 1716 and (detail) the water-damaged
first entry on the page

Plaque marking Robert Paterson's
birthplace, still in situ
(note the erroneous date)

Closeburn Castle, the tower house of the
Kirkpatrick family

Ruins of Closeburn Old Parish
Church, built 1741: Paterson
was reputedly involved in its
construction

Drumlanrig Castle, Thornhill,
the home of the Douglas family,
ancestors of the present owner,
the Duke of Buccleuch and
Queensberry

Spedlins Tower, immediately north of
Corncockle Quarry, near Lochmaben

The Harkness family grave, Dalgarnock Cemetery, Thornhill (note the cursive inscription, reputedly by Paterson)

The Nithsdale Martyrs' Cross, also in Dalgarnock Cemetery

Carved tablestone support, reputedly by Paterson, Closeburn churchyard

Ruins of Morton Old Parish Church, the Patersons' former place of worship

The original Caldons Wood gravestone, now in Newton Stewart Museum

The 1980s replacement, in situ

The harbour at Kirkcudbright, Barscobe Castle in the middle

The gravestone of Robert Lennox, Covenanter, in Girthon Old Parish churchyard

The tablestone of Covenanters William Hunter and Robert Smith, St Cuthbert's churchyard, Kirkcudbright

The reputed site of the Patersons' former home in Balmaclellan, now a machine parts store

Tablestone of Covenanter Robert Grierson, Balmaclellan churchyard

The Paterson family grave in Balmaclellan churchyard, including that of Elizabeth Gray

Balmaclellan Church: the Patersons would have worshipped here after 1768

The list of Paterson's funeral expenses as transcribed by Thomas Boyle Grierson in 1857

The pencilled note contained within the pocketbook

Headstone in Bankend of Caerlaverock Parish churchyard commemorating Robert Paterson

Old Mortality's leather pocketbook, on display in Dumfries Museum

Old Mortality statue:
Balmaclellan Church

Old Mortality statue:
Dumfries Museum

Old Mortality statue:
Newton Stewart Musuem

CHAPTER SIX

THE COVENANTING TRADITION

Departure

In August 1758, following a period in which he was increasingly absent from his family, Robert Paterson left home entirely, not returning to his wife and children for some ten years. Thus began the peripatetic life of carving and repairing gravestones and memorials for which Paterson is chiefly known and which continued to the end of his life. This much we know from the testimony of his son, the additional evidence of Joseph Train and the commemorative stones that form a trail through the churchyards of the south-west of Scotland. What is less clear are the motives which led to Robert's departure and the influences which brought them about.

As we saw in the first chapter, there are problems with the version of Robert Paterson's story presented to Sir Walter Scott by Joseph Train. Significant elements of it rely on a transcription of documents which Train received from Paterson's son, the contents of which were printed almost *verbatim*, as part of the Introduction to the 1830 edition of *Old Mortality*. The letter from Robert junior which contains the most relevant details of his father's life was dated 20 September 1827 but its contents were not relayed to Scott until April 1829.* During the intervening period Train had apparently gathered a lot more information but it is suspicious that he chose to paraphrase the original letter rather than sending it directly to Scott or at least enclosing it with the new material.

One of the most crucial differences between the two texts is the interpretation put upon Paterson's covenanting beliefs as a motive for his subsequent travels, of which Train makes a great play but his son does not mention at all. Ramage, in whose history of Drumlanrig and the Parish of Morton the letter from Paterson junior is quoted in full, noted this discrepancy and said that it "somewhat dimmed... the air of romance which Sir Walter Scott has contrived to throw over his character."[1] It did not, however, prevent him from going on to relate the standard interpretation, which he dressed as "local tradition" but which was in fact taken from Train's version of events.

Without direct access to Robert junior's letter, Scott knew no better but he was sufficiently wary of Train's reports to ask his editor to leave out certain aspects of the story of Old Mortality contained in the missive of 31 March 1829. Towards the end of Train's letter he referred to the so-called 'Napoleon connection' with another of Paterson's sons, John, which is dealt with in more detail in Chapter Eight. Scott, himself a master of embellishment, knew when a story was too good

---

* The sequence of correspondence is described in more detail in Chapter One and relevant notes.

to be true and judiciously omitted this tale from the introduction to the 1830 edition of his novel.

Train's motive in putting a Covenanter 'gloss' on his portrayal of Robert Paterson, if that is what he did, was clearly to perpetuate the interpretation of the stonemason's life's work that was crucial for the purposes of Scott's novel. Without it, Scott did not have a rationale for the new introduction to his novel, the opening chapter or for its title, a situation Train could hardly allow his patron to be in. Robert junior, on the other hand, despite living in an area that was the heartland of the religious struggles of the late seventeenth century, was, by the 1820s, part of a modern Scottish society that was slightly embarrassed by what it saw as the coarse 'fanaticism' of those times. For that reason he might have attempted to put a more rational gloss on his father's story.

Before examining the interpretation of Paterson senior's motives in more detail, it would therefore be useful to understand its context.

The Covenanters

'Covenanters' is a term that applies to people within the Presbyterian faith, the form of Protestantism that emerged from the Scottish Reformation, who subscribed to a series of National Covenants during the seventeenth century. Presbyterianism was founded upon a literal interpretation of the Bible as the Word of God. The thirty-nine articles of the Westminster Confession of Faith, which were part of the Solemn League and National Covenant of 1643, were regarded as the *principal subordinate standard*, ie. instructions for the observance of the religion that were subordinate only to the Bible.[2]

In the middle part of the century the supporters of the Covenant comprised many powerful figures in the Scottish establishment, the landed gentry and middle classes who were, in the absence of Charles I in London, in effect the rulers of the country. During the English Civil War they sided with the Parliamentary forces in return for promises to uphold the faith in Scotland (hence the 'Westminster Confession'), helped to defeat the king in battle and handed him over to Oliver Cromwell. (They changed sides when the English executed Charles, a Stuart monarch, and tried to restore his son to the throne in return for the same promises, paying the consequences when Cromwell's forces marched into Edinburgh. All of which only demonstrated the determination of the Scots to retain their chosen religion.)

Following the Restoration of 1660, Charles II again promised freedom of worship but circumscribed the way in which the Presbyterian Church was allowed to operate in Scotland. In particular, through the Act of Presentation and Collation of 1662, he introduced a system of church governance through bishops, similar to the Church of England and known in Scotland as Episcopacy or Episcopalianism.

Under this system church ministers, previously chosen by local heritors and vetted by the kirk session, were henceforward only licensed to preach by the state-appointed bishop.

A majority of the population were prepared, reluctantly, to accept the change, along with a few other, relatively minor, differences between the two forms of religion (for example, the Lord's Prayer, recited at the end of Episcopalian masses, was a new introduction). But this particular imposition was a sticking point for many Presbyterians for whom the interference of the state in their affairs, a principle known as Erastianism, was unacceptable.

Adherents to the National Covenant believed that the government of the church should rest on a hierarchy starting with individual members of the congregation who were encouraged to read and understand the Bible for themselves and take personal responsibility for their own consciences and their relationship with God. The congregation, armed with this self-awareness, then elected local representatives to the parish kirk sessions which were in turn represented, or had a voice in their representation, at district presbyteries, provincial synods and finally the national general assembly.[3]

Within this relatively simple and democratic structure, however, there was plenty of scope for ambiguity, even after Episcopalianism was removed from the state religion and, over the next twenty five years, as each side became more entrenched in their positions, the term 'Covenanter' came to apply less and less to those who espoused Presbyterianism *per se* and more and more to those who stood for a particular form of Presbyterianism. Eventually, Covenanters came to be known for their intransigence in espousing quite narrow definitions of church governance, religious observance and moral behaviour.

During the period 1660 to 1679, some 300 existing ministers - about a third of the total in Scotland – stood firm to these principles, refused to accept the authority of the local bishop for their positions and were consequently ousted from their churches. Many took to the fields and began to hold open-air 'Conventicles', often quite large and involving several thousand followers at a time, rather than seek the licence of the state to preach.

The south-west of Scotland was disproportionately represented amongst the numbers of parishes which were effectively 'deprived' of a minister in this way. Mark Jardine[4] notes that forty-eight per cent of parishes in the south of Scotland generally were deprived for not conforming to Episcopacy but that figure disguised relatively few abstentions from parishes in the east and central parts of the country rising to over fifty per cent in the western and south-western counties, such as around Kirkcudbright and Dumfries, and to nearly seventy-five per cent in Ayrshire, Lanarkshire, Renfrewshire and Wigtownshire (in Galloway).

Many of the more radical ministers also hailed from this part of the country. David Dickson of Irvine in Ayrshire and Samuel Rutherford of Anwoth, near Kirkcudbright, had already been leading supporters of the Covenants in the 1640s. Some of the infamous preachers of the later part of the century included Alexander Peden, also from Ayrshire who preached in Galloway; John Welch of Irongray in Nithsdale; John Blackadder, whose church was in Troqueer, near Dumfries; and, most significantly, Richard Cameron, originally from Fife but who was a pupil of Welch. Cameron preached across the south-west and set a new standard for extremism when he effectively declared war on the state in the Sanquhar Declaration, which he posted in the centre of the town in upper Nithsdale in June 1680. He was captured and killed by government troops within a month of the incident but his reputation, and that of his supporters, for uncompromising adherence to the Covenants was by this time firmly established.

The south-west of Scotland, and parts of Dumfriesshire and Galloway in particular, thus became a focus for the dissemination of opposition to the way in which the state sought to proscribe religious worship. Meanwhile, the government of the day, by reacting in a heavy-handed fashion through fines for non-attendance at church, imprisonment or exile and even military reprisals, did little to appease the situation and much to inflame it with the result that the more obdurate ministers found a ready audience for their sermons and even for insurrection.

In 1666, for example, provoked by the presence of government troops posted to keep the peace following the outbreak of war with Holland, mobs in St John's Town of Dalry and nearby Balmaclellan, both in the Ken Valley, north of Castle Douglas, sparked a series of violent episodes which were collectively known as the 'Pentland Rising'. A rapidly escalating number of peasants and local gentry, citing adherence to the Solemn League and National Covenants, formed an army which overpowered the troops, marched on Dumfries (where they found and captured their commander, Sir James Turner) and then on Edinburgh before eventually being overpowered by another government force.

Instead of learning their lesson, however, the authorities undertook severe reprisals: several prisoners were taken back to their home towns in the Glenkens, to the north-west of Dumfries, or to Dumfries itself, for public execution. These incidents later gave rise to a rash of memorials for the martyrs thus created.

Repression prompted reaction and further repression in a deepening spiral of violence which saw a number of pitched battles between the opposing sides in the 1670s before descending into guerrilla war and culminating in the so-called 'Killing Times' of 1683-85. (The exact dates differ depending on the source for, and the range of, the atrocities - on both sides - to be included in the definition.) At the height of the conflict, between the end of 1684 and the summer of 1685, there were eighty summary executions and many hundreds more dissenters were deported to the colonies.[5] The hardening government position was prompted to a great degree by domestic political conspiracies in England and threats of invasion from abroad, especially at the beginning of the reign of James VII (an avowed Catholic) in 1685, but the pretext continued to be attendance – or suspected attendance – at non-sanctioned masses and the refusal of local residents to swear allegiance to the Crown.

On the government side, the main protagonist in the systematic hunting down and execution (with or without trial) of Covenanters was John Graham of Claverhouse, a former soldier in William of Orange's army in the Netherlands and so notorious that he was the only 'real life' character to be depicted as such in Scott's novel. Claverhouse was involved in many of the pursuits and ambushes of Covenanters in the south-west and led a number of pitched battles against their forces, even after his royal master fled the country in 1688, and died in his cause a year later.

Within Dumfriesshire and Galloway, however, the two principal government agents were Sir Robert Grierson of Lag and Colonel James Douglas of Morton, his brother-in-law (Grierson was married to Lady Henrietta Douglas). Grierson's base was near Dunscore in Nithsdale but, according to the later Covenanter martyrology, he was instrumental in several of the more notorious executions of the whole region during the Killing Times, for which services he was created a baronet by James VII. He is also supposed to be the inspiration for the character of Sir Edward Hugh Redgauntlet in Scott's eponymous novel, set in a period after the 1745 uprising. Grierson was still alive and living a public life in 1727, when his niece Susan Grierson married Sir Thomas Kirkpatrick, despite attempts by local Covenanters to have him tried for his role in the persecution of members of their families.[6]

Colonel James Douglas was the brother of the first Duke of Queensberry and is also implicated in several infamous incidents of the 1680s, including one or two which – if the martyrology is to be believed – amounted to assassinations of fugitive Covenanters. Douglas' views of the Covenanters, expressed through his actions, were clearly shared by his brother who, in addition to his many landed titles, was until 1682 Justice-General of Scotland under Charles II and subsequently the High-Treasurer, retaining that title briefly under James VII. Upon the occasion of the latter's accession, the duke pinned his colours to the mast by telling the king that he hoped

> "effectual ways will be fallen upon for destroying that desperate, fanatical and irreclaimable party (the Covenanters) who have brought us to the brink of ruin and disgrace, and are no more rebels against the King than enemies of mankind, wretches of such monstrous principles and practices as past ages never hears and those to come will hardly believe."[7]

The Legacy

The violence came to an end with the Glorious Revolution of 1688-89 in which James VII was toppled by his cousin and son-in-law, William of Orange. As part of the Revolution Settlement of 1690, Episcopalianism was proscribed and Presbyterianism was re-established within the Church of Scotland on the basis of the thirty-nine articles of the Westminster Confession. Though doctrinal differences remained, most Covenanters largely accepted the settlement position as the least worst option, the alternative being to oppose and potentially weaken the new state, allowing James VII to return with a Catholic or Episcopalian church. As proof of this a Covenanter army helped to defend the new government by standing up to and defeating Jacobite forces at Dunkeld, on the edge of the Highlands.

That said, old animosities died hard and grievances continued to ferment, not least among the United Societies, a network of prayer groups formed after the death of Richard Cameron but adopting his militant outlook. Their members, known collectively as 'Society People' or 'Cameronians', were small in number – perhaps five or six thousand in total – and concentrated inevitably in the rural south-west, comprising tenant farmers and tradesmen. However, their influence at the local level was strong due, firstly, to the importance of the kirk as the focus for community activity and debate in Scotland and, secondly, to their ability to think and argue for themselves in a way that was remarkable for people at this level of society at the beginning of the eighteenth century and a testament to the grass roots nature of Presbyterian teaching.

Using skills honed by years of practice in interpreting the words of the Bible, the Cameronians were able individually and in family groups to wield disproportionate influence over neighbours and within local congregations, continuing to lead dissension within the ranks of the church (and several schisms, well into the nineteenth century) and generally to oppose authority where they felt it was misguided.

In the southern parishes of Galloway in the 1720s, for example, many tenant farmers suffered eviction from their arable land to make way for an early form of enclosures in which beef cattle could be raised. This led to a popular rising by what were known loosely as the 'Levellers of Galloway' (because they 'levelled' the farm dykes which were being built to enclose the cattle) who for a few months in 1723 and 1724 caused alarm amongst landowners who called for military intervention.

The rising centered once again on communities within the Ken Valley, including the area around St John's Town of Dalry, and was eventually put down. However, as part of the disruption, those involved invoked the Solemn League and National Covenant, a nebulous attempt to demonstrate the righteousness of their cause and opposition to the establishment by reference to a movement which had fought successfully for their rights in another context.

More significantly for our story, the Cameronians also clung tenaciously to the memory of their erstwhile companions who had fallen during the struggles of 1682 to 1685. Through the United Societies they sought recognition of their martyrdoms and resolved to begin identifying their gravesites or places of execution and to mark them with appropriate monuments. This resulted in the publication of *A Cloud of Witnesses* in 1714,[8] the anonymous, largely anecdotal and poorly printed work of a committee which was nonetheless hugely popular and went through several reprints during the eighteenth century.

This clamour for commemorating the Covenanters was reinforced by other writers who, ironically, had the objective of defending the established Presbyterian church against the radicals by demonstrating that it too had grown through the sufferings of an earlier generation. Robert Wodrow, who published *The History of the Sufferings of the Church of Scotland from the Restoration to the Revolution* in 1722, was a minister in the Church of Scotland and a member of the moderate party. Wodrow decried the persecutions of the Covenanters on the one hand but on the other castigated extremists, like the Cameronians, for leading people down paths that led to excess and violence (what he called "enthusiasms") that were ultimately fruitless. In the process he produced some four volumes of persecutions and martyrs which, while still largely anecdotal, considerably added to the pantheon.

The net effect of these and other publications of the period was to surround the Covenanter martyrs with a romantic glow that persisted for many in rural Scottish society through the eighteenth and well into the nineteenth centuries, even if it was an increasing source of embarrassment to an educated, urban elite that had passed through the Scottish Enlightenment.

The Local Context
In the interpretation of Robert Paterson's story that has come down to us from Joseph Train, the stonemason is seen as an unreconstructed Cameronian from the outset, although how he is supposed to come by his views is not explained. To illustrate this, in the information supplied for the later edition of Scott's novel, Train related the tradition of Paterson's unsympathetic reaction to the arrival of retreating Highland soldiers in Morton parish in the aftermath of the 1745 rebellion.

The rebellion was led by Bonnie Prince Charlie, the grandson of James VII, who supported the claim of his Catholic father, James (the 'Old Pretender' who had led the 1715 rising), to the throne. In this version of events, stragglers from the

'Young Pretender's' army "plundered" Paterson's home and took him as a hostage on their journey north. This because he had apparently remarked to them that

> "their retreat might easily have been foreseen, as the strong arm of the Lord was evidently raised, not only against the bloody and wicked house of Stewart, but against all who attempted to support the abominable heresies of the Church of Rome."[9]

Based on this story, which would have occurred only a couple of years after the Patersons' arrival in Morton, Train concluded that "Old Mortality had, even at that early period of his life, imbibed the religious enthusiasm by which he afterwards became so much distinguished."[10]

The story has a strong factual basis in that the retreating Highland army, including Bonnie Prince Charlie himself, did indeed pass through the parish towards the end of December 1745. A detailed account of their passage was supplied in letters, written only days after the event, to the third Duke of Queensberry (residing in London at the time) by his Commissioner of Supply, James Fergusson of Craigdarroch. Fergusson's main concern was about the damage caused to Drumlanrig by Jacobite forces who billeted themselves at the castle on the evening of 23 December. In apologetic tones, he recalled for the benefit of his lordship how:

> "When they came here they laid straw the whole rooms for the private men to lye on, except your Grace's bed-chamber (where their Prince lay) and a few rooms more. They killed about 40 sheep, part of your Grace's and part of mine, most of them in the vestibule next the low dining-room and the foot of the principal stair, which they left in a sad pickle, as they did, indeed, the whole house. Under the gallery they keepd several of their horses, which they made a shift to get up the front stair. They have destroyed all the spirits and most of the wine in your Grace's cellars—of both which there was a considerable stock and very good, which has been laid in gradually since I came here—a good deal of hay, and what corn they could get, all my ale and spirits, and other provisions. They have broken several chairs and tables, melted down a good deal of pewter by setting it upon the fire with their victuals, cai'ried away a good deal of linen and several other things, which I have not yet time to know particularly."[11]

The main body of the retreating army left Drumlanrig, and the region, promptly the next morning. But three days later stragglers were continuing to pass through the area. On 1 January 1746 Fergusson wrote again to his master explaining how:

"...On 26th December last, eight men and five women who had straggled from the rear of the Highland army were brought here prisoners. The afternoon before they were plundering near Durisdeer, and were attacked by fourteen country people, seven of whom only were armed. They fired upon the people, but did no execution, upon which those who had guns returned their fire, and wounded most of the Highlanders, and before they had time to draw their swords ran upon them and knocked them down."[12]

Durisdeer is only four miles or so from Gatelawbridge and soldiers travelling up the east side of the valley from the south would almost certainly have passed within a few hundred yards of Paterson's home to reach it, if not past the front door itself. Those mentioned above, or another group at around the same time, could therefore have taken him prisoner and, at the very least, Fergusson's account does suggest that the Highlanders were taking what spoils they could as they passed through the countryside, probably unpaid and unfed. But whether Robert took the opportunity to utter his deprecations to them as they did so and whether they plundered his house and took him prisoner as a result is less clear.

In Robert Paterson junior's account,[13] on which Train's was based, the story is more straightforward. Elements of the retreating Jacobite army did indeed call at the family home and take his father into their charge, he remembered, evidently recounting a tale passed down from his mother, Elizabeth. The latter, he added, "got a great fright" believing she would never see her husband again. However, it appears that the soldiers only wanted him to conduct them to the nearest smithy, "where they could get their horses shod," and asked "many questions", as soldiers passing through a part of the country that was alien to them would be wont to do. Having secured their objective, Paterson's son recalled, the Highlanders "set him safely at liberty."

So Train's embellishments of the story, including a direct quote for which there could not have been a contemporary source, are almost certainly fabrications intended to create the impression that Paterson already held strong Covenanting beliefs in his late twenties, which is questionable. Another reason for doubting that Paterson was predisposed to a Cameronian outlook at this date is the fact that he had not been averse to taking a lease from, paying a rent to or indeed working for the descendants of those whom Covenanting tradition dictated had been instrumental in the violent oppression of their forebears.

Both the Queensberry and the Kirkpatrick families could be cited in this respect. In addition to the graphic accounts of Colonel James Douglas' activities, the *Cloud of Witnesses* portrayed Thomas Kirkpatrick, the first Baronet and grandfather of Paterson's contemporary who resided at Closeburn House and who had helped him to acquire a lease on his quarry, as a persecutor during the Killing Times.

Sixty years later, as we have seen, such traditions would have been important for those who kept the faith, reinforced by the marriage of the third Baronet to Susan Grierson, niece of the infamous Grierson of Lag.

The truth was, of course, more complicated than this. Powerful families like the Douglases could not afford to oppose, or to be seen to oppose, the monarch without losing their titles - and the basis for their increasing wealth – unless they were prepared to go all the way and openly rebel. William Douglas, having secured a dukedom for his family and his future heirs, was quite prepared to support in return James VII's anti-Covenanting crusade in 1685 and his brother likewise.

A year later, however, he resigned from the government, disapproving of James' increasingly open Catholic sympathies and, by the outbreak of the Glorious Revolution he was in London, waiting in attendance upon William of Orange. At the latter's coronation, alongside that of his wife, Queen Mary, the first Duke affirmed his loyalty to the new king, saying he would now stand "not only for the King, but will concur in Presbytery (sic) as now fitt for the King and the Nation."[14]

Circumstantial evidence suggests that Sir Thomas Kirkpatrick, the first Baronet, was also less hostile to the Covenanters than the traditions of the Society People would have it. Like William Douglas, he had to be careful to be seen to be supporting the government as appropriate and was in fact one of the county commissioners appointed to work with Colonel James Douglas during the height of the repression in the 1680s.[15] But he also saw himself, in the patrician sense, as a local Laird first and foremost and tried to steer a middle course between his duties to king and country and his responsibilities for his tenants.

Thus Sir Thomas received his baronetcy from the Stuarts under Charles II and retained it under James VII, but he later also retained the favour of William II (of Scotland, III of England) for his support for the Church of Scotland after the Revolution of 1689. In addition, his second wife, whom he married in December 1672, was Sarah Fergusson, daughter of John Fergusson of Craigdarroch, a staunch supporter of the Covenanters and himself briefly a fugitive during the Killing Times.[16]

Simpson, in his *Traditions of the Covenanters*, written in the middle of the nineteenth century, went further and recounted the story of Sir Thomas hiding local Covenanters from the troops which had occasion to search his land. Simpson added that the first Baronet kept a "confidential domestic servant whom he employed to give warning to local Covenanters seeking shelter on his property."[17] However, without further evidence for these stories, we are treading into anecdotal territory similar to that occupied by Joseph Train.

The important point is that it seems unlikely that Robert Paterson would have understood or indeed concerned himself with such subtleties when he moved to Morton, preferring instead to concentrate on the development of his new business and the upbringing of his family – as we saw in the last chapter. The fact that he did so, despite the widely known recent history of the area and its landowners during the Covenanting struggles, with its ongoing antagonisms, lends further support to the notion that Paterson was not deeply imbued in those beliefs, or even an avowed Cameronian, at least at this stage of his life. However, these subtleties and antagonisms would become crucial factors in his eventual decision to become more closely involved with Covenanting history, and for the itinerant lifestyle to which it would lead.

The Influence of Local Traditions
The open air 'conventicles' which had been held as a necessity by ousted ministers during the 1660s to 1680s continued to be conducted, albeit less frequently, during the eighteenth century as a way of commemorating the earlier period of struggle. They were attended largely by the fundamentalists, those who adhered to a narrow interpretation of the early Covenants such as the Cameronians who, by 1743, had seceded from the established church to form their own, Reformed Presbyterian Church. But they also appealed to a wider audience.

Writing of his visit to Drumlanrig in 1724, for example, the novelist Daniel Defoe said that he witnessed a "field meeting" or Conventicle in the area in which a Presbyterian minister, Mr John Hepburn, "an old Cameronian", preached to a gathering of some 7000 people, "all sitting in rows on the steep side of a green hill, and the preacher in a little pulpit made under a tent at the foot of the hill..." He added that Hepburn preached for seven hours with an intermission of only half an hour, and that many of the people had come from as far as fifteen or sixteen miles away.[18]

Such events were also often held to commemorate a specific martyr on the site of their execution and to coincide with the erection of a monument to the individual concerned – an occasion which would have interested a wide section of the local community. Given the fugitive nature of those who were hunted down, these sites were – and can still be found – in remote areas of the countryside.

In the information supplied by Joseph Train to Sir Walter Scott, he stated categorically that Old Mortality was "a most strenuous supporter" of the tenets of the Cameronians and that he "made frequent journeys into Galloway to attend their conventicles"[19] such as those described above. Train noted that Paterson carried with him on these occasions gravestones from his quarry at Gatelawbridge to "keep in remembrance the righteous". He explained that, "as his enthusiasm increased, his journeys into Galloway became more frequent" until he eventually neglected even his family and decided to devote himself entirely to the cause.

By contrast, Robert junior said, in his first letter to Train, that his father saw the commercial opportunities inherent in the lack of sandstone (he referred to "freestone") in Galloway and consequently of material for gravestones "or any to work them." Paterson senior therefore conducted "repeated trials of carrying gravestones into Galloway and selling them," all of which "answered his expectations of a profitable concern." According to his son, he made "several trips into Galloway", sometimes leaving his apprentice, Sandy Rae, to finish a stone. But, he announced without explanation, "some time about August 1758, my father neglected to return to his family."[20]

Once again, while the core events related by these two versions of the story appear to have a factual basis, there is a clear difference of interpretation of Paterson senior's motives. And, once again, the truth lies somewhere in between, with Paterson being more likely to have been influenced in his beliefs over time and as a result of constant contact with local families and their traditions.

Morton and the parishes surrounding Robert's home were rife with stories and families that had connections with the Covenanters and even some survivors old enough to have suffered persecution in the 1680s. According to Hewison,[21] one such was Andrew Ker of Shiel, near Carronbridge, at the mouth of the Enterkin Pass, the scene of an ambush of government soldiers escorting prisoners to Edinburgh in July 1684. Following this affair, the government issued a proclamation requiring local parishes to draw up lists of fugitives from their homes who were accused of being "rebellious & unnatural subjects", ie. Covenanters.

The list for Morton parish contained no fugitives but named several families described as "recusants and those lybele for phanatical and church disorders within the samene" (sic) and gave their locations.[22] The return for Closeburn and Dalgarnock parish was similarly detailed but listed several fugitives. This included members of the Harkness family who were famous, or notorious, Covenanters, hailing from remote moorland farms to the east of the parish.

Whole generations of the family, men and women, devoted themselves to the cause and one or two individuals were synonymous with some of the most infamous clashes in the Covenanting lexicon. These included James 'Long Gun' Harkness and his brother Thomas who actually led the Enterkin Pass ambush. Thomas Harkness was among those perpetrators who were later captured by Claverhouse and subsequently hanged in Edinburgh but James escaped, returned home and lived until 1723. His descendants were still very much part of the local congregation during Robert's time in the parish.

Closer to home, just across the river in Closeburn parish, was Crichope Linn: a deep, wooded sandstone ravine which, according to tradition, was formerly used by Covenanters (and possibly other refugees from the law) as a hiding place or retreat. It was used as the basis for the "Black Linn of Linklater" in the closing scenes of *Old Mortality* and, despite its dark and damp environment, was described by Scott as the kind of place where Covenanters "judged it safer to face the apparitions by which the place was thought to be haunted, than to expose themselves to the rage of their mortal enemies."[23] The linn itself is a waterfall which might have been used for baptisms, as were many similar sites across the region.

More generally, while the *Cloud of Witnesses* only identified four records of martyrs from Dumfriesshire and five from Galloway, such publications spurred local people to recollect and research their own family histories and to find ways of commemorating the involvement of their ancestors in the insurrections of the seventeenth century. As we have seen, the pantheon was added to considerably by Wodrow and others within just a few years. A cross erected in Dalgarnock old churchyard in 1928 listed the names of some fifty-seven martyrs in Nithsdale alone. Over time, commented Hewison,

> "Every parish in Nithsdale had a green mound or two, with or without a slab, to tell that 'a kindly Scot lies there' for Christ's Crown and Covenant."[24]

In Morton and a number of the surrounding parishes, according to Hewison's fieldwork, Robert Paterson was not only commissioned to provide and inscribe stones for the new martyr monuments but also to repair the stonework and freshen the inscriptions of those which had been previously erected. In the course of these commissions, or simply as a result of rubbing shoulders with his neighbours, Paterson would have met the family members concerned and learnt and transcribed the stories they had to tell of their ancestors, and of local traditions generally, so gaining a deep insight into family histories, the tragedies of individual Covenanters, their principles and those of the movement as a whole.

"So his stonecraft brought him where rural hearths rang with the exploits of the hillmen"[25], Hewison concluded. It also meant that his work was itself contributing to their legacy and to its perpetuation at a key moment in the movement's history.

Examples of Paterson's work in Nithsdale, like any other stone monuments, suffer from the neglect of centuries but many have been preserved by lack of development in what is still a very rural area and some, especially those relating to Covenanters, have been carefully preserved or recarved by devotees. In addition to those gravestones in Morton old churchyard which are contemporary with his time there, they include the gravestones of the following individuals or families with Covenanting associations:

- the Harkness family of Mitchellslacks and Locherben, as already described, who are commemorated on several headstones in Dalgarnock Cemetery, a mile or so south-west of Thornhill.
- Daniel MacMichael, brother of 'Black' James McMichael, one of the organisers of the Enterkin Pass rescue in July 1684, who was killed in a separate incident six months later and whose grave is in Durisdeer churchyard, north-east of Thornhill. According to his epitaph, McMichael, an apparently frail individual, was apprehended following the raid on a conventicle being held near Morton Castle and was on his way to Edinburgh for trial when his captors decided he was too weak to travel and shot him instead, his body being brought back to Durisdeer for burial.
- John Mathieson of Closeburn, a follower of the preacher Alexander Peden, who was arrested in June 1684, gaoled and tried in Dumfries and transported to the colonies. He returned within a year and subsequently served in the Cameronian army before retiring to Closeburn and dying in 1716. His graveslab is propped up against a wall within the ruins of the old parish church. It had to be recut as the inscription names the person who apparently betrayed Mathieson to the authorities and his descendants are reputed to have smashed the original as a consequence.
- William Smith of Hill, near Moniaive, to the west of Thornhill, a nineteen-year old farm tenant's son who is buried in nearby Tynron churchyard. He was arrested in March 1685, held for refusing to answer his interrogators (and probably for refusing to swear an oath of loyalty) and summarily shot upon the orders of Sir Robert Laurie of Maxwellton, one of the county commissioners serving under Colonel James Douglas. According to legend, Smith's father was originally forced to bury his son under the front door of his own house so that he would be constantly reminded of the deed when he crossed the threshold, a fact alluded to in the inscription on the gravestone in Tynron.

Many of the Nithsdale martyrs are commemorated on Gatelawbridge sandstone, often with reference to Revelations xii, 11 ("And they overcame him by the blood of the Lamb, and by the word of their testimony; and they loved not their lives unto the death") as well as other inscriptions and phrases, as if conforming to a single committee's choice of words or those of a single sculptor. As can be seen from the above list, they are often not contemporary with the deaths of the people commemorated or the events surrounding them and for the most part are post-1714. It seems that Robert would therefore have had a hand in carving many of these or at least in recarving them.

Patronage
And if the influence of the past was not enough to indoctrinate Robert, arguments over church principles still raged in the present, sufficient to remind the congregation of what their ancestors had fought for.

Much of the controversy of the seventeenth century had sprung from the issue of 'patronage' or who should appoint the ministers. The Revolution Settlement had left this power in the hands of the kirk session but pressure from local landowners and heritors generally led to a change of heart by the government which was also conscious of a looming crisis over the succession. With James VII's son waiting in the wings to claim the throne from childless Queen Anne, they passed the Lay Patronage Act of 1712 as a way to keep landowners onside: from the heritors' point of view, it was only right that they should have a say in the selection of a minister and in the running of local church affairs if they were being asked to contribute to its maintenance and upkeep.[26]

However, as we have seen, in many areas these contributions were not forthcoming or at least were not as high or regular as local people thought they should be. Aside from the principle that their hard-fought for ability to run matters in their own communities was being revoked, parishioners also felt that the lack of financial contributions by heritors brought into even more doubt their right to appoint ministers. Through the 1720s and into the 1730s, as landowners started to exercise their newly restored power upon the death, retiral or removal of ministers, replacing them with ministers of their own views or social station, the church once again became the focus of disputes.

Nationally, this led to a number of secessions from the established church and new churches being set up at frequent intervals, causing friction between rival local communities. More often, attempts by landowners to impose their own minister on a parish were met by legal objections, delaying new ministers from taking up their posts for months or even years, or simply by physical intimidation, preventing the new ministers from entering the church or saying mass. Such events sometimes necessitated military intervention, especially as the century progressed and agricultural tenants and craftsmen vented the anger they were feeling over pressure from other directions, including agricultural improvements, commercialisation of rents and loss of land to enclosures.

Morton parish was not immune from these pressures which, although they did not come to a head until just after Paterson's departure, illustrated differences between the outlook of the church establishment and the underlying sentiments of many of his fellow parishioners.

Early in 1759 the local minister, Archibald Little, found or was offered a new position in Kirkpatrick-Irongray parish, in the south-west of the county. In the minutes of the local presbytery, the entry for 1 March 1759 includes the record of a petition against the 'transportation' of the minister, signed by six kirk elders, a heritor (Robert Dalziell, the only landowner in the parish aside from the Duke of Queensberry) and forty-four heads of families.[27] The Reverend Little departed nonetheless and in May the presbytery wrote to the Duke to advise him of the vacancy, urged on by the elders of Morton parish itself who wrote again in June asking that the vacancy be filled as soon as possible.[28]

In due course Robert Aitken of Coilsfield was proposed by the Presbytery at the suggestion of the Duke but this was met in December by a petition from the single other heritor and fourteen heads of local families on the grounds of patronage. The petition, entitled 'Reason why some heads of families in the parish of Morton refuse to sign a call for Mr Robert Aitken to be their minister' was accompanied by another paper from Robert Dalziell himself entitled 'A protest and testimony by the residing heritor and some heads of families in the parish of Morton'. The latter stated:

> "We undersubscribers judge it our duty for the Glory of God and the exoneration of our own consciences to protest against patronage as contrary to the word of God and Presbyterian principles which we stand solemnly engaged to maintain..."[29]

The Presbytery decided as a result to call Robert Aitken to be "tested" prior to appointment and in March 1760 they convened to hear the prospective new minister recite and answer questions on several passages from the Bible plus be examined in Latin and Greek. Satisfied with his performance, the Presbytery agreed to appoint Aitken as minister and decided to meet again in Morton Church to announce this to the local parishioners. A further written protest was received from the parishioners at this decision but no further objections were made when the members of the Presbytery reconvened in Morton in April 1760 – some fourteen months after the previous incumbent had given notice - and announced Robert Aitken's appointment at the doors of the church.

Aitken duly served as minister in Morton parish for twenty-four years but the repercussions of his appointment could be seen in the declaration of faith which a new group of kirk elders were required to swear upon their ordination in May 1764. The candidates, which included the schoolmaster, Andrew Greggan, made clear their

> "...protestation against all the Deflections and Corruptions of the ...church either in doctrine, worship, discipline or government, particularly against the rigour or severity of Patronage as having no foundation in the word of God, and being disruptive in many cases of the peace and tranquility of the church and productive of many evils..."[30]

A Middle Way
The available evidence suggests that Robert Paterson was not a 'dyed in the wool' supporter of the Covenanters when he first came to Gatelawbridge, as Joseph Train would have us believe, nor even particularly zealous when it came to church

matters. But nor is it easy to believe, as his son suggested, that he gave up his family and what appears to have been a thriving stonemasonry business, at the age of forty-two, simply in order to earn a living by selling headstones to remote hillside settlements. In fact it is undeniable that Paterson, in embarking upon his travels, would have relied for a significant part of his business on families and communities with Covenanting associations and that he must have had an interest in and a desire to perpetuate them through the means at his disposal.

It therefore seems more likely that Paterson's interest in the Covenanters, and his development into a Cameronian – if that is what he eventually became – was nurtured slowly, over the course of his fifteen years or so in Morton parish and subsequent travels, as the result of a specific set of circumstances. Robert's trade as a stone quarrier and mason meant he offered material and skills that were increasingly in demand as part of a burgeoning economy but particularly to meet the developing fashion for headstones and similar memorials. His chosen base was, if not at the heart, very much within a region with strong Covenanting traditions whose residents, in parallel with the fashion for headstones generally, were eager to commemorate their own martyrs.

These two factors brought him, more so than most, into regular contact with Covenanter families, their stories and beliefs and were probably what prompted him to seek out the company of similar followers of the faith further afield: initially out of curiosity but, from the available evidence, with a commercial instinct as well. In the course of his travels, with blocks of sandstone strapped to the back of his pony, and in long hours spent at his craft in lonely churchyards, Paterson might then have developed his apparent obsession with the Covenanters to the exclusion of all else.

Notes

1   Ramage, CT, *Drumlanrig Castle & the Douglases*, 1876, *op cit.*
2   CG Brown in *Religion*, a chapter within *Modern Scottish History 1707 To The Present,* Ed. A Cooke, I Donnachie, A MacSween & CA Whatley, 1990.
3   Stevenson, D, *The Covenanters: The National Covenant & Scotland*, , Saltire Pamphlets, 1988
4   Jardine, M, *The United Societies: Militancy, Martyrdom and the Presbyterian Movement in Late-Restoration Scotland, I679 to I688*, University of Edinburgh, 2009.
5   Stevenson, *op cit*
6   Gladstone, J, *The Kirkpatricks at Capenoch, 1727-1846*, Transactions III/15/85
7   From an unattributed article about the Buccleuch and Queensberry families, written around 1884.
8   Thomson, John Henderson, *A Cloud of Witnesses for the Royal Prerogatives of Jesus Christ: Being the Last Speeches and Testimonies of Those who Have Suffered for the Truth in Scotland Since the Year 1680*. Oliphant, Anderson & Ferrier, Edinburgh, 1714.
9   Train to Scott, Letter of 31 March 1829, *op cit.*
10 *Ibid.*
11 Whitelaw, JW, *Some Incidents in Nithsdale during the Jacobite Rising of 1745*, Transactions II, Vol.11, 117, 1894
12 *Ibid*
13 Ramage, *op cit.*
14 Cited in Hewison, JK, *The Covenanters*, vol 2, 1913.
15 Jardine, M, *op cit.*
16 Kirkpatrick, C, *Records of the Closeburn Kirkpatricks* , Glasgow 2003
17 Simpson, R, *Traditions of the Covenanters; or, Gleanings among the mountains*, 1867.
18 Defoe, Daniel, Letter 12, 'South Western Scotland' from *A Tour Through The Whole Island Of Great Britain 1724-26*, Webb & Bower, 1988 Edition.
19 Train to Scott, Letter of 31 March, *op cit.*
20 Ramage, CT, *op cit.*
21 Hewison, J K, *op cit.*
22 The lists, submitted by local ministers to government representatives in Dumfries in October 1684, are reproduced in *Covenant and Hearth 1684-91*, Shannon, RA, 1973
23 Scott, W, *Old Mortality*, Penguin 1975
24 Hewison, JK, *op cit*
25 Hewison, *op cit*
26 Brown, CG, *op cit*
27 Penpont Presbytery records for 1756-67, including records for Morton Parish, NLS CH2/298/4.
28 *Ibid*
29 *Ibid*
30 Morton Kirk Sessions 1714-1810.

CHAPTER SEVEN

TRAVELS

The Evidence of the Stones
At this distance in time, it is not possible to trace with any precision the route or routes which Paterson travelled once he adopted his itinerant lifestyle. All that we can do is to piece together a very broad picture from the snippets of information which are available and, of course, the evidence of the gravestones which he inscribed so distinctively.

One of the first Covenanter's stones said to have been carved by Paterson outside Nithsdale was originally located in Glen Trool, a steep-sided valley about twenty miles north of Newton Stewart, in the west of Galloway. The area is more famous as the location of one of the battles of the Scottish Wars of Independence, led by Robert the Bruce, this one being a relatively minor skirmish which took place in April 1307. It is commemorated by an inscription on a giant boulder perched on a hillside overlooking the west end of Loch Trool.

The nearby Caldons headstone, by contrast, is on the base of the valley, hidden in a midge-infested Forestry Commission woodland of the same name. Reached by a thin, riverside path through the trees, it commemorates the execution of six men by troops led by Colonel James Douglas for refusing to swear an oath of loyalty at the height of the Killing Times in January 1685. (Legend has it that a seventh man, a brother of two of the men killed, escaped by diving into the loch and standing up to his neck amongst the reeds while troops searched around him.)

The headstone stands alone, enclosed within a stone wall about 5 feet high, and is carved in white granite with lettering in the same style as Paterson used. The original, which was damaged by vandals and replaced in the 1980s, was carved from sandstone that local museum staff analysed and determined had come from Gatelawbridge. Fully repaired, it now hangs in Newton Stewart Museum: a beautiful, if relatively small example of the stonemason's craft.

To this day, although some have been recut or even replaced, many other headstones and monuments conforming to Paterson's style can be spotted in churchyards across the region. In addition to those already described in Nithsdale – for which there is a significant absence following Paterson's departure, according to Hewison[1] – the list of parish churchyards which can be demonstrated to contain his work includes those in:

- Penpont, mid-Nithsdale
- Sanquhar, upper Nithsdale

- Kirkchrist and St Cuthbert's churchyards, to the west and east, respectively, of Kirkcudbright
- Anwoth and Girthon, either side of Gatehouse of Fleet
- Balmaghie, north of Castle Douglas
- Balmaclellan, further up the Ken Valley, of which more later, and
- Kirkmaiden, just below Portpatrick, the furthest west and south in the region.

Using these locations as a very rough template, Paterson's travels therefore appear to have taken him out along the Solway coast, from Caerlaverock and Dumfries west to Wigtown, Glenluce and the Rhins of Galloway, as well as north into the mountains around Newton Stewart and the Glenkens. This conforms with Robert Paterson junior's claim that "there are few churchyards in Galloway, and especially in Wigtownshire, but he wrought in".[2] Indeed, other, documentary, evidence – discussed below – appears to confirm that this area was the focus of Paterson's activity for the rest of his life.

However, traditions also exist of Old Mortality having a hand in headstones and monuments in parts of the south-west of Scotland outside Dumfriesshire and Galloway. Joseph Train asserted that "the labours of Old Mortality, in the course of time, spread over nearly all the lowlands of Scotland",[3] though he only mentioned Ayrshire in addition to the areas already noted, while Robert junior added that "large portions of his (father's) handycraft are yet to be seen."[4] Given the plethora of Covenanting sites and memorials in this region, it would seem highly likely that Paterson paid a visit to the areas concerned – possibly including parts of Lanarkshire and even the Central Belt - although, without a detailed study like that undertaken by Hewison in his native county of Dumfriesshire, there can be less certainty about his presence in any given parish.

Another tradition asserts that Paterson travelled as far afield as Dunnotar, in Aberdeenshire, on the north east coast of Scotland. There a memorial in the local churchyard commemorates nine Covenanters who died while being held in the dungeons below Dunnotar Castle in May 1685. The stone in question certainly appears to be a good example of Paterson's style, with incised Roman lettering, employing ligatures extensively and concluding with reference to the Book of Revelations (although, in this case, the numbers have been wrongly transposed as chapter eleven, verse twelve).

As we saw in Chapter Five, however, this style of lettering was quite traditional while inscriptions for the more significant Covenanting memorials – such as this - were often governed by a committee; so the qualities of the inscription do not guarantee Paterson's involvement. The tradition that Paterson carved the stone *in situ* is also based solely on Sir Walter Scott's description, in his novel, of seeing Old Mortality actually working on the stone and his later claim to have met Paterson during a visit to the area in the summer of 1793.[5] For example, John Duncan, a noted nineteenth century botanist who was born in Dunnotar in 1794, a year after the event supposedly took place, recalled for the benefit of his biographer being taken round the churchyard by his mother when he was young and having the stone pointed out to him because of its Covenanting associations. Writing in 1883, his biographer then added with hindsight that it was the one "at which Sir Walter Scott first saw 'Old Mortality'."[6] *

This tradition must therefore be treated with suspicion given its distance in time from the event and Scott's obvious lack of knowledge of who he is supposed to have encountered: in the letter in which he made the claim it is obvious that he knew little of Paterson's life story (or even his first name[†]) despite his detailed portrayal of the character of Old Mortality for the purposes of the novel. If true, however, the story would also suggest that Paterson made a round trip of at least four hundred miles, on foot, to visit the site at the age of seventy-seven.

Written Evidence
We are on surer ground with other, documentary sources which back up the evidence of the stones or otherwise place Paterson in areas where there is an established presence. In Robert Paterson junior's account of his father's life, given to Joseph Train, he said that a year after his disappearance, ie. in 1759 or 1760, his mother sent one of her sons, Walter, in search of his father. Young Walter, then aged about twelve, could not possibly have been expected to guess entirely his father's location or search fruitlessly for him through the whole region. So, reading between the lines, we can assume that Elizabeth had a good idea of the part of the region on which her husband was concentrating, either because he continued to stay in touch with his family, however infrequently, or because the bush telegraph worked well enough in rural areas in the eighteenth century to give her sufficient information to direct her son. And indeed, according to Robert junior, his brother does appear to have found their father quite quickly, albeit with "some difficulty".[7]

In his version of events, Joseph Train typically embellished this story saying that Walter only found his father after "traversing the whole of that extensive district, (ie. Galloway) from the Nick of Benncorrie to the Fell of Barullion".[8] More helpfully, however, he added that the boy found him "working on the Cameronian monuments" in Kirkchrist churchyard, just to the west of Kirkcudbright, a claim for which the evidence is not given but which chimes with the pattern of Paterson's travels generally and the further evidence which follows.

---

* William Jolly, the biographer, notes that Old Mortality had died by the time that Duncan was five years old. There is no mention, as some have suggested, of Duncan actually meeting Paterson himself.
† In the letter, written in 1827, Scott says he met "John" Paterson "some thirty years ago", a reference to a tour of north-east Scotland he is known to have made in 1793.

The natural assumption is that Elizabeth sent her second eldest son in search of his father in order to ask him to return. Given the obvious zeal with which her husband was now approaching his mission, she may nonetheless have already realised that this was a forlorn hope and instead may have had broader designs. By this time Walter would have been about the age of his father when he first left home to become apprenticed, and Elizabeth may therefore have sent her son away in the hope that he would embark on a similar path. It would also have been one less mouth to feed.

If the latter *was* Elizabeth's motive then it worked because, according to Robert junior, his father "did not allow (Walter) to return, but put him to school and afterwards learned him the trade of stone-cutter".[9] The fact that Walter Paterson became a stonemason is confirmed by the inscription on his own gravestone in which he is described as a "stone engraver" but also by several other sources. In 1784, for example, years after his mother and his siblings had relocated to Balmaclellan and Walter had settled down with his own family, the minutes of a meeting of the local heritors show him being awarded the commission to build the village's first dedicated schoolhouse. The new, stone-built, slate-roofed property, for which he charged £27, was completed in July 1785.[10]

Other documentary evidence places Robert Paterson in or near Kirkcudbright during the 1760s. According to court sessions records for the burgh,[11] in October 1766 one John McGowan, a shoemaker, brought an action against "Robert Patterson (sic), stone-cutter", claiming payment of six shillings for the hire of a pony some five years previously, ie. shortly after he was reunited with Walter in nearby Kirkchrist churchyard. According to the record, in Paterson's absence the court at first decreed in McGowan's favour but then reopened the case upon receipt of a petition from him, suggesting that he was still in the area or passed through on a regular basis. In his sworn statement Paterson said he had only agreed to pay four shillings for a journey from Kirkcudbright to Wigtown and thence to Glenluce and this the court accepted, reducing his debt accordingly.

After 1768, as already mentioned, the Patersons relocated to Balmaclellan. While this does not seem to have limited Robert Paterson's wanderings, it did nonetheless provide him with a base within Galloway and once again fixes the pattern of his travels within the broad area already described. Indeed, Paterson's presence in Balmaclellan is one of the very few for which there is eyewitness corroboration and, more valuably, a description of his appearance. According to Ramage, writing in 1876, a by then elderly inhabitant of the village, Mrs Janet Clement McLellan, remembered seeing him on one occasion when she was just "a young bit lassie" and Paterson himself around eighty years old. She said:

> "He was a gey, droll-looking old body. He was riding on a wee bit white pony, had on an auld hat hanging over his lugs, and the pony was ganging unco slow."[12]

The only other confirmation of Paterson's movements during his later life comes from documents found in his possession and returned to his family after his death. As discussed in Chapter One, these were passed to Joseph Train by Robert junior, probably in September 1827, along with "the Mallet and Square used by (his father) in following his avocation."[13] Like the tools of Paterson's trade, the original documents have long since disappeared, although a leather pocket book, or wallet, which might once have contained them, is now held by Dumfries Museum, together with a short handwritten note, in an unknown hand, attesting to its authenticity.*

Train, however, transcribed the contents of two of the documents in his letter to Sir Walter Scott of 31 March and they were reproduced in the introduction to the 1830 edition of the novel. One of the documents relates to Paterson's burial and is discussed in Chapter Nine. The other was a note, apparently in Paterson's own handwriting, with the location and date "Gatehouse of Fleet, 4th February, 1796" which records his debts to one Margaret Chrystale for a number of items incurred while staying in her lodging house. They include:

• four shillings and a penny "To drye Lodginge for seven weeks";
• three shillings and fourpence "To Four Auchlet of Ait (oat) Meal" (a measure, usually sold by the sack, approximating to about four stone or fifty-six pounds in total); and
• a shilling and threepence "To Six Lippies of Potatoes" (about ten or eleven pounds).

In total the debts amounted to fifteen shillings and fivepence, of which five shillings and fivepence were recorded as unpaid, possibly remaining so at the time of Paterson's death, a practice to which he was clearly not averse. The fact that Robert was able to pay off ten shillings of the debt suggests nonetheless that he was both living and working in the area during the period concerned.

Gatehouse of Fleet lies just a few miles west of Kirkcudbright and therefore very much within the part of Galloway on which Paterson had concentrated for the previous forty years. It was then a new town, planned and developed towards the end of the eighteenth century by James Murray of Broughton on the back of cotton manufacture and its trade. Paterson is thought to have carved headstones in both Girthon and Anwoth parish churchyards, just a couple of miles either side of Gatehouse.

In an addendum to his letter to Scott of March 1829, Train recounted an anecdote concerning slanderous accusations which Old Mortality is supposed to

---

* The Museum record says that the note is by Robert junior but it seems more likely to have been written by a third party much later in the 19th century . It refers to his son, Thomas, having "lived and died" in Balmaclellan and to his son, also called Robert and "also a lover of justes" (sic). The pocket book may have been donated by Jane Murray, Thomas Paterson's wife, who died in 1929.

have made in the presence of local children in Girthon churchyard about the red tinge of wooden utensils produced by their grandfather, the village cooper. He implied that they came from the coffins of people buried in the churchyard there, an accusation over which the cooper is supposed to have taken Paterson to court to get a retraction. Whether true or not, the anecdote was used by Scott in the introduction to the 1830 edition of the novel and showed, he said, that the old man "loved an innocent jest" even if "his jests were of a melancholy and sepulchral nature".

Margaret Chrystale hailed originally from the area around Dundrennan, in Rerrick parish, about five miles south-east of Kirkcudbright, where she was baptised Margaret Chrystel.[14] In 1796 she was thirty years old and married to James Rain, a merchant. The couple had married in her parents' parish but she had evidently followed her husband to the burgeoning new port of Gatehouse where they became tenants of the Broughton estate.

Townhead of Enrick was one of a cluster of houses on the eastern edge of Cally Park, between Gatehouse and Girthon, and apparently big enough for Margaret to set up the lodging house of which Robert Paterson made use. She gave birth to her first child later the same year and had at least four more children in the property, finishing her days as a tenant at nearby Cally Mains, the estate farm, according to her gravestone,* at the age of fifty-one.

Returning briefly to the list of Paterson's debts to Margaret, it is worth noting that they included ninepence for "Three Chappins of Yell (ie. tankards of ale) with Sandy the Keelman". This is footnoted in Scott's introduction to explain that Sandy the Keelman was a dealer in 'keel' or chalk with which farmers marked their sheep. In Train's original letter to Scott he had provided a lengthy paragraph of background to the man, who was apparently a well-known character from Nithsdale[15]. He said he worked from a place called Kelly Cleugh, near Drumlanrig Castle (there are several still existing candidates for the place name in an area that was then well known for its limestone quarries) and was "great cronies" (ie. friends) with Robert Paterson. It is intriguing to think of Paterson, supposedly a staunch teetotaller with a taciturn reputation, meeting up with a former friend from his days at Gatelawbridge to pass away an evening in their declining years with a few glasses of beer.

The Roads Taken

The natural assumption from hearing of Robert Paterson's apparently extensive travels during this period, ie. the last forty years of the eighteenth century, is that the road network in the south-west of Scotland had much improved and that

---

* Margaret, her husband and five children who predeceased her are commemorated in a single grave in Gatehouse churchyard. Her name by the time of her death had become Christal. She died in 1817 and was followed by her husband a year later.

transport conditions were generally good. This was only partly true: conditions continued to improve as the century and economic conditions progressed but, especially at the outset of Paterson's period of travels, the picture was still very mixed and in some, remoter areas, would remain so until well into the nineteenth century, long after his death.

John Clerk of Penicuik, one of the Duke of Queensberry's accountants, kept a diary of his travels between the Duke's estates during the first half of the century. In 1735 he recorded the details of a journey from Drumlanrig into Wigtownshire via Dalry, a route which Paterson himself would begin to use frequently some twenty-five years later and which, with several variations, was of great antiquity. It formed part of the established pilgrimage route between Edinburgh, Newton Stewart and Whithorn (the site of St Ninian's first Christian settlement in Scotland) and was used by James IV on two occasions in the late fifteenth century as well as by Mary Queen of Scots in 1563.

Clerk appears to have travelled for part of his journey on foot, staying with the Fergussons at Craigdarroch, outside Moniaive, and then at Dalry. The next morning, reaching the Water of Ken, he took a horse as the water was too high to ford and travelled south to Brig of Dee, a crossing point north of Castle Douglas, from where he continued to Minigaff, east of modern Newton Stewart. He completed the journey of twenty-nine miles in five hours he said, stopping at various viewpoints along the way. Of the first stage, following the course of the river Ken, he said it was a "Monstrouse bad road" and described the whole journey as being rough and mountainous. "The pass called the Saddle Loup" he added, "is here about 4 miles from Minigaff. Nothing in the Alps is worse." Conversely, he was pleased to note that "The way between Drumfrise (sic) and Kirkcudbright is very fine."[16]

From about this period onwards, however, the minutes of the Commissioners of Supply for Dumfriesshire, the Stewartry of Kircudbright and Wigtownshire are increasingly informative and show in detail the pattern of development of the road and bridge network. During the 1730s and 1740s a 'wave' of bridges was commissioned and built and lengthy contracts began to be let for their upkeep from the 1750s. This meant that travellers, even if they had to use roads of dubious quality, could at least approach the crossings to which they led with greater confidence. By 1763 the Military Road from Carlisle to Portpatrick had also been completed, the first road of any quality or significance outside the main towns since the Romans and an event which spawned a period of more intense roadbuilding generally.

That said, by the mid 1760s most 'roads' within the region were still really tracks or drove roads, only allowing travellers a choice of routes on foot or horseback: which of course suited Paterson's chosen mode of travel entirely. The pony with which Paterson is usually depicted as travelling was in fact a Galloway Pony or Nag, a small but distinct local breed of horse noted for its strength and stamina but also for its speed if ridden.

The breed's origins are hazy but its fame by the late middle ages was widespread. It was referred to in Shakespeare's *King Henry the Fourth Part II* when he wrote, "Know we not Galloway Nags" and is thought to be the breed used by the Border Reivers when raiding into England in the sixteenth century.[17] Daniel Defoe also remarked upon "the low breed of horse which is much prized for its stamina and strength" during his travels through south-west Scotland in the 1720s.[18]

The Galloway Pony was perfect for Paterson's purpose of carrying heavy loads, such as pre-carved headstones, on rough tracks into remoter settlements, as well as for carrying him back, if he needed to return home more speedily. All contemporary descriptions of Paterson, especially in his old age, mention him in the company of a pony or small horse and it is how he was nearly always caricatured in images and statues in the nineteenth century. By this time, however, the breed had fallen from favour and was losing position to larger draught animals which were more suitable for agricultural work.

Meanwhile, the roads on which Paterson and other travellers relied continued to improve. Despite the commutation of labour in favour of taxes, the Statute Labour Act, previously mentioned in Chapter Three, was proving ineffective and in 1780 an act of Parliament allowed the conversion of a landowner's liability for making improvements to money payments so that repairs could be carried out by contractors. In addition, the various Turnpike Acts of the late eighteenth century allowed roads to be tolled (tollbooths were built every six miles or so) so that investors could get a guaranteed return on their capital.

This saw the development of many new and higher quality roads through the 1790s. Travelling through Nithsdale in 1792, for example, the Galloway-born author Robert Heron praised the local highway as "... one of the best roads I have ever travelled, level, smooth, dry and of sufficient breadth. Turnpikes have been erected at proper distances."[19] It is unlikely that Paterson would have used such roads himself but the relief from having to build and improve longer distance roads allowed parishes to concentrate their resources on improving local roads so he may, albeit in his later years, have benefited indirectly.

The Travelling Tradition
Regardless of the motives for Paterson's wanderings, his itinerant lifestyle was not so very unusual for the age in which he lived. At a time when rural society in particular was essentially localized, both as a contributory factor towards and a consequence of poor roads and slow transport, travellers of any description were positively welcomed for the news they brought of the outside world, the

opportunity which they presented for socialising in an otherwise unchanging routine and, of course, the essential wares which they carried with them for purchase. Every village and hamlet received and even looked forward to visits from tradesmen and hawkers of every conceivable ware, wayside preachers, soldiers on their way to or from foreign campaigns or just plain travellers with news to tell.

The travellers themselves were also from the same or similar classes as the people they served with their news or trade. The settlements they visited were largely self-sufficient and existed barely above subsistence levels, a situation in which the travellers also existed, relying – if they were salesmen - on credit from the urban wholesalers from whom they bought their goods and hoping for payment of debts from the individuals and families to whom they sold them. The principal difference between them being that one worked hard in a single location while the other suffered the iniquities of travel in eighteenth century Scotland – poor roads, long miles on foot, harsh weather and the potential for robbery or violence.

There were a number of different types of traveller and some famous examples of each in various parts of the country. We have already heard of the example of Sandy the Keelman, Paterson's friend who sold chalk. In the south-west of Scotland in the 1720s another well known character was Patrick Walker, a preacher and storyteller of a Covenanting persuasion who wandered the countryside in the company of a white pony.[20] Yet another character was Dugal Graham, known as the Bellman of Glasgow until his death in 1780.[21] Before being employed as such, he had travelled the countryside around Ayrshire and Lanarkshire during the 1750s and later selling 'chapbooks' or pamphlets.

A chapbook could be anything from a political or religious tract to printed songs and ballads to a hefty volume of quality literature or an almanac or atlas. As we have already seen, while Scottish rural society in the early part of the century was essentially illiterate and reliant on oral traditions, it was sufficiently literate – certainly by the middle of the century – for healthy debates to be conducted in many homes around the reading and interpretation of the Bible.

The chapbooks that were sold by pedlars like Dugal Graham were equally popular. But they nonetheless contained, more often than not, less lofty material, had very rough woodcuts for illustrations and had more racy titles such as *Peden's Prophecies, Leper the Tailor, Jocky & Maggie's Courtship* or *The ravishing, dying words of Christina Ker, who died at the age of 10*. By the middle of the eighteenth century, it has been estimated that some 200,000 such books and pamphlets were sold each year by booksellers in Scotland, many of whom were travelling salesmen.[22] Graham himself was apparently a hunchback of dwarfish proportions who also travelled with a pony.

Salesmen of this variety sold, of course, a much wider range of goods than just books and were known collectively as 'chapmen', the word meaning "a petty or itinerant merchant or dealer". As well as calling at hamlets, villages and individual cottages, they could be found – licensed and unlicensed - at annual fairs and weekly burgh markets. The eighteenth century, and especially the mid to later part of the century, was their heyday: as the population grew and the economy prospered and people demanded a more varied range of products for their home and work.

According to a study produced by Roger Leitch in 1996,[23] citing contemporary sources he showed that mounted and pedestrian chapmen were numerous by the 1780s, travelling with large packs and lodging at rural cottages and farmhouses. Those with more substantial packs, he said, occupied a role similar to mobile shops in rural areas today. He confirmed that, as a rule, these itinerant salesmen received as much food as they could eat and were often given supplies to last them to their next destination. And he added that "they were usually a well-informed class of men (and women) and played a useful role in circulating the news of the day, telling of matters political, ecclesiastical, and domestic."

The goods the chapmen offered for sale also became more diverse and luxurious. From the 1740s onwards Scottish linen became more prevalent and in demand and bolts of cloth were frequently the staple stock of chapmen travelling into remote glens and coastal settlements. Other increasingly popular items included metalwares such as tea kettles, or imported goods such as English cloth, silk for the better off, and cotton on the back of the newly emerging industries such as at Gatehouse, whether in the form of threads or locally manufactured goods, as well as a more eclectic range of products such as wigs, candlesticks and goose quills for writing. Gravestones of good quality sandstone would have been in equal demand.

Making a Living
In his letter of 1827 to Joseph Train[24] Robert junior made no mention of his father's income but, as we saw in the last chapter, explained that his original forays into Galloway to 'test the market' for headstones suggested that it could be a "profitable concern." By the late 1760s, he added, "his business lay now entirely in the churchyards," which meant, however, that he could not make enough money to stay long in one place and "it therefore behoved him to travel".

As usual, Train, in relaying Robert junior's sentiments to Scott, went a step further and claimed that Paterson's "task of repairing and erecting gravestones (was) practised without fee or reward".[25] Old Mortality, he said, was able to eke out an existence by lodging with families sympathetic to the Covenanting cause, paying for their hospitality in kind by erecting, repairing and inscribing gravestones or memorials to local martyrs in churchyards and remote hillsides. At each household, Train added, "he was gladly received as an inmate of the family", the implication being that he learnt during his stay with each family a little more of local Covenanting traditions, helped in their commemoration and was told about another martyr who had fallen in the next valley, which warranted a visit and maybe a stone to mark the spot, continuing in this vein for some forty years.

The truth, once more, lay somewhere in between. It is clear from the description of Paterson's travels above that he led a hand-to-mouth existence, living frugally, often paying for items on credit and leaving a trail of debt behind him. Especially in his old age, Train says, the "religious wanderer" appears to have been very poor. It also seems to be a mode of living that he suffered by choice, as can be seen from his conscious decision to leave behind his business in Gatelawbridge and, later, to continue on his travels even once his family were firmly established with businesses and income of their own in Balmaclellan and, Train adds, "most anxious to keep their father at home".

Yet Paterson did not always rely on charity or work without some payment, as we have seen from his recorded outgoings in Gatehouse and the income which he must have earned to pay for them, at least in part. Train also acknowledges that Paterson must sometimes have made use of commercial lodging but without admitting that the old man must have gained some financial return for his work in order to have survived. In particular, he would have had to pay for stone for new headstones, the basic material of his trade, given that he no longer made use of his own quarry.

Robert junior addresses this issue by explaining that his father purchased his gravestones – or at least the stone from which to carve them - from other quarries in the region, notably Locharbriggs, near Dumfries, but also from Whitehaven, in Cumberland, "as he found most convenient." The latter source refers to St Bees and Kirklinton sandstone, a red sandstone quarried just a few miles south of the port of Whitehaven which in the second half of the eighteenth century was one of the largest in Britain, after London and Liverpool.

On a clear day the St Bees headland is easily distinguished on the southern horizon from any vantage point on the Kirkcudbrightshire coastline and Whitehaven was an important *entrepôt* between the Scottish Solway ports and trade with the rest of the world. The ready access which it gave to a source of building stone for towns and villages in Galloway provides a possible clue as to why Paterson might have spent so much time in and around the port of Kirkcudbright.

It is nonetheless important not to exaggerate the scale of this trade which until the end of the eighteenth century would have been quite tiny and only destined for the more grand building projects of the region. According to the Old Statistical Account, even by 1792 imports through the port of Kirkcudbright were mostly of cotton and coal. The total cargo carried by the twenty-eight ships registered to the harbour was only 1,053 tons (a small modern freighter could be expected to carry five to ten times this cargo by itself), with corn and grain being the principal exports, plus some manufactures.[26]

Given his limited requirements, Paterson might therefore have bought a few individual stones from ships entering Kirkcudbright or Gatehouse harbours with blocks to spare or, more likely, from the stone ballast which many ships traditionally carried to give them stability when sailing empty to pick up a cargo. Ships plying the Atlantic routes in particular often carried such stone in the form of carved headstones as they had a ready use for the residents of their intended destination.

However, although it is not mentioned by Robert junior, who after all was not a stonemason, it is equally likely that his father acquired his stone from the handful of outlying sandstone quarries in Galloway itself. Before the advent of industrial quarrying of granite in the nineteenth century, the traditional building material of this part of Scotland was whinstone, a sedimentary stone also known locally as greywacke. The quality of this stone differed from location to location as it was often formed by mud flows covering other types of rock hundreds of millions of years ago, meaning the size of the grains varied and the rock itself could only be crudely shaped. This was acceptable for rough building stone but not for fine carving such as that which sandstone allowed and which was required for headstones.

The few sandstone quarries which existed in the region were mostly to be found as outcrops along the coast, rather than as commercial quarries. The rock was available to those who knew where it was and could expose, cut and carry it away. Indeed, its rarity and value often meant that the quarries in question were exploited for major, local building projects, as required, and then closed.

This was the situation along the Rerrick coastline, south-east of Kircudbright, where sandstone had been produced by ancient volcanoes which had dried the surrounding stone to the extent that it had crumbled as sand and then solidified. The resulting strata had been exploited by Cistercian monks in the twelfth century to build nearby Dundrennan Abbey, at the time one of the richest abbeys in Scotland, perhaps second only to Melrose. It dominated the local area for four centuries until its suppression following the Reformation, after which it was left to go to ruin. Over the intervening two centuries much of the stone had been pilfered as ready-made building blocks for other properties, including Kirkcudbright Tolbooth.

According to the Old Statistical Account, in the 1790s, however, there were still a number of 'freestone' quarries along the Rerrick coastline:

"The coast everywhere abounds with freestone, which has been much in request of late, for the ornamental parts of some of the most elegant houses, both in this and neighbouring parishes."[27]

It therefore seems very likely that Robert Paterson would have availed himself of one if not both of these sources of sandstone for his profession – whether freshly quarried from the ground or removed from the once magnificent buildings of Dundrennan Abbey – and that this was another reason for his regular presence in the area.

In this context, it is worth noting that the sandstone for the construction of Dundrennan Abbey, which Paterson might also have used, came from Netherlaw Glen, just a few hundred yards north of Netherlaw House. The latter was a large coastal property facing Abbey Burnfoot, a rocky cove from which Mary Queen of Scots is said to have set sail for England, never to return, in the late spring of 1568*. It was also where John Chrystal, the father of Paterson's future landlady, Margaret, was for a long time the gardener. This could have a been a coincidence or, in one of those distant personal connections that makes local history so rewarding, it could have been the origin of their relationship.

Whatever the truth of the matter, Robert junior's confirmation that his father continued to acquire stone for his business tells us that there must still have been a commercial aspect to his activities. Picking up private work here and there, as a peripatetic stonemason, may therefore have helped to subsidise his otherwise altruistic undertakings. In this chapter we have therefore established roughly where and by what means Paterson travelled and existed, and demonstrated that his itinerant lifestyle would not have been regarded as that unusual in rural settlements of the period, even if the motive for his wanderings was more unconventional.

---

* The adjacent Port Mary is the traditional location for Mary's embarkation but local historians now lean towards Abbey Burnfoot as being closer, more sheltered and having a history as the local fishing port. Netherlaw House was pulled down in 1939 to make way for the MoD Firing Range which still covers the area.

Notes

1   Hewison, JK, *op cit.*
2   Ramage, CT, *Drumlanrig Castle & the Douglases*, 1876, *op cit.*
3   Train to Scott, Letter of 31 March 1829, *op cit.*
4   Ramage, CT, *op cit.*
5   Letters of Sir Walter Scott Vol.X, 1828-31, ed. HJC Grierson - Letter to Rev. John Carslaw of Airdrie, 22 May 1827.
6   Jolly, William, *The Life of John Duncan: Scotch Weaver and Botanist*, , 1883.
7   Ramage, CT, *op cit*
8   Train to Sir Walter Scott, 31 March 1829, *op cit*
9   Ramage, CT, *op cit*
10 Heritors' minutes for Balmaclellan 1782-95.
11 Robinson, Joseph, 'Old Mortality in Kirkcudbright', Transactions, II, Vol.20, 157 (1907/8).
12 Ramage, CT, *op cit.*
13 Train, Joseph, *Brief Sketch of a Correspondence with Sir Walter Scott commencing in the year 1814*, 1st July 1833 (National Library of Scotland, MS 3277).
14 Register of Births, Deaths and Marriages, Rerrick Parish
15 Joseph Train to Sir Walter Scott, 31 March 1829, *op cit*
16 Sir John Clerk's Journey into Galloway in 1735, Prevost, WAJ, *Transactions* III, Vol.42, p133 (1963)
17 Grierson, James C, 'The Galloway Pony Or Nag', Transactions III, Vol.77, p233 (2003)
18 Defoe, Daniel, *A Tour Through The Whole Island Of Great Britain 1724-26*, *op cit.*
19 Heron, Robert, *Observations made in a journey through the western counties of Scotland*, 1793.
20 This example comes from Graham, H G, *Social Life In Scotland In The 18th Century*, A&C Black, 1937.
21 *ibid*
22 *ibid*
23 The interpretation of chapmen, and much of the material on them which follows, comes from a detailed report entitled *'Here chapman billies tak their stand': a pilot study of Scottish chapmen, packmen and pedlars*, Roger Leitch, Proceedings of the Society of Antiquaries of Scotland, vol.120 (1990).
24 Ramage, *op cit*
25 Joseph Train to Sir Walter Scott, 31 March 1829, *op cit*
26 OSA, Stewartry of Kirkcudbright, Kirkcudbright parish, 1792.
27 OSA, Stewartry of Kirkcudbright, Rerrick parish, 1793.

CHAPTER EIGHT

HIS FAMILY

Elizabeth (1)

When Paterson set out from Gatelawbridge on his travels in 1758 he left behind his wife, Elizabeth, and at least five children, ranging in age from thirteen to less than two years (assuming that Francis died in infancy). According to the youngest of his children, Robert junior, he did not return to his family for ten years, ie. until 1768, when he uprooted them to Balmaclellan, in the heart of Galloway. How his wife and family coped during this time is not clear but we can perhaps piece together a picture from the available evidence.

During the period in question, Robert junior said, his father made "but few remittances" of money to his family, the implication being that he didn't leave them completely destitute.[1] Certainly there is no record from the kirk or presbytery session minutes of Elizabeth seeking or being given alms, food or loans by the church although recipients were rarely singled out by name. Apart from one or two instances of special pleading by specific individuals or their relatives, poor money in Morton appears to have been distributed automatically each month to a handful or more deserving causes already known to the minister and parish elders.

But neither is there any reference in the church records to the apparent scandal, to modern eyes, of Paterson leaving his family for so long. As we have seen, the kirk in the eighteenth century was quick to interrogate and, where found guilty, reprimand parishioners for failing to meet strict moral standards. This happened particularly in the case of non-marital relationships: kirk session minutes are full of references to men and women being taken to task for sex outside marriage, even going so far as to question couples whose first child appeared too soon after their marriage.

However, there was also a clear expectation that men should take responsibility for the children they produced, both morally and to prevent their families from becoming a burden on the parish. There are several – often long-running – descriptions in the kirk session minutes of men being brought to account for relationships which had left their erstwhile lovers with child. Eventually, after much evidence on either side, the fathers were usually forced either to marry the women in question or to provide for them financially.

Despite that, Elizabeth's situation is not anywhere mentioned, suggesting on the one hand that she and her family did not become a liability on the local poor relief and on the other that the relationship within the marriage was therefore of no concern to the church. As we have seen in previous chapters, Paterson's absences from home were also by 1758 a regular and known feature of his life and business, fitting into a contemporary tradition of travelling tradesmen and other forms of itinerant commerce and therefore perhaps not regarded as being so unusual - as long as his wife and family were catered for, or were providing for themselves.

In this respect, aside from the bonus of any 'remittances' which her husband may have continued to send home, we can assume that Elizabeth's strategy would have been simply to subsist on her own land, earn income as best she could for herself and her family and reduce outgoings as much as feasible. There is no suggestion that she fell back on her own parents or other close relations or friends for direct assistance. Also, having been brought up as a gardener's daughter and starting work as a servant in a busy household at the age of fourteen, she was not a stranger to hard work.

As far as income was concerned, and as was typical for many homes of the period, Elizabeth and her daughters would probably have earned money from spinning wool and knitting clothes. Both Elizabeth and her eldest daughter, Margaret, aged thirteen, would already have derived an additional household income from this source prior to Robert's departure. Janet, aged five, would soon be similarly employed, if she wasn't already. As the Reverend James Smaill commented in the Old Statistical Account for Dornock Parish, near Annan,

> "...the expense of maintaining the family will (usually) exceed the man's earnings... but the deficiency is generally made up by the wife's industry, by her working in hay-time and harvest... and by her spinning through winter and spring..."[2]

Following Paterson's departure, we can assume that she and her daughters stepped up their efforts – an initiative for which they would have had a certain amount of local encouragement.

At this period, prior to the development of sheep farming to meet mass markets for meat, wool was valued as one of the principal by-products of the animal and the basis for a significant cottage industry across Scotland. Collected from the household's own herd, bought from neighbours, or simply paid for at market, it was combed, braided and spun into yarns to produce hodden grey (coarse, undyed cloth), plaidings (dyed and therefore more decorative cloths) or blankets, shawls, stockings and the like. The combined efforts of much of the local female population of many parishes (and many men in winter, depending on their occupation) produced considerable quantities of these materials which could then be sold at market, either to local individuals or to wholesalers.

David Loch, a merchant and shipowner from Leith who visited Nithsdale in 1776 on a tour of inspection on behalf of the Board of Trustees for Fisheries, Manufactures and Improvements in Scotland, commented on the situation in "Thom-Hill" (Thornhill):

> "Here are four markets or fairs in the year, and much coarse linens and woolen (sic) goods are sold at these fairs, as people from England come to them. A good deal of woolen yarn is likewise spun here, which goes to Kilmarnock for the carpet manufactory. A number of looms is employed in these parts, and the proprietors send all their goods to Thom-Hill markets..."[3]

By the mid-eighteenth century, moreover, the industry was receiving considerable support in the form of national and local subsidies and Nithsdale was regarded as one of the centres of excellence for woollen products which resulted. Commenting on the woollen industry at Sanquhar, a few miles up the valley from Gatelawbridge, David Loch noted that:

> "His Grace the Duke of Queensberry... contributes £40 annually... which are given as premiums to the people in this neighbourhood, in order to promote industry; and, by this means, the spinning of wool and knitting of stockings, which they do better here than anywhere in my tour (Aberdeen excepted)."[4]

This achievement was the result of several years of subsidies from both the Queensberry Estate and the Board of Trustees, each for their different reasons. The Duke, as we saw earlier, was trying to keep skilled workers on his estates, maintain rent levels and specifically to establish the town of Thornhill, with its market for local produce; while the Trustees, on behalf of the Government, were promoting Scottish industry in general.

An advert printed in Edinburgh on behalf of both bodies in July 1763 - while Elizabeth was still living in the area – promised "premiums for promoting the spinning of woollen yarn, the knitting of woollen stockings and weaving of woollen cloth in the Presbytery of Penpont..." of which half were paid by the Trustees and half by the Duke. The premiums were intended to cover the cost of "utensils, ground and buildings", as appropriate, and the advert went on to promise:

> "To the journeyman-weaver, married or who marries within 2 years of this date and who makes the best quantity of woollen cloth proper for Thornhill Market, a house lately built in Thornhill...to him and his heirs provided they continue the business of weaving, rent-free for 19 years and weaving utensils to the value of £6 sterling..."

Similar, lesser value inducements were offered to the next two best weavers with further rewards of materials, equipment and apprenticeships to others who showed promise.

Other prizes were offered for the best examples of "spinning yarn" and "knitting the best or most woollen stockings" in various age brackets. They included "up to 7/- for the boy or girl below 8 years of age for knitting the best or most woollen stockings" and up to thirty shillings for the best families in each category as well. As we have seen already, this formula proved successful for the Queensberry Estate and we can safely assume that Elizabeth and her daughters also made the most of the opportunity to earn a living for themselves.

John

Elizabeth appears to have been equally enterprising in her efforts to reduce her outgoings. Within a couple of years of her husband leaving she despatched, in quick succession, her two eldest sons to gainful employment elsewhere as soon as they were of age. In about 1759 or 1760, as we saw in the last chapter, Elizabeth reduced the number of mouths she had to feed when Walter became apprenticed to his father. Then, at about the same time, according to a second letter which Robert junior sent to Joseph Train in May 1829,[5] she sent her oldest boy, John, to live and work with a relative on a farm near Dumfries. And therein lies a fascinating story.

John Gray was a cousin of Elizabeth's and a tenant at Laghall Farm, near Glencaple, on the Nith estuary south of Dumfries. A couple of years after his father had departed on his wanderings, Robert junior said, Gray paid a visit to Elizabeth and her family in Gatelawbridge. Presumably because he thought that his cousin was finding it hard to cope with her family on her own, he offered to take John – then aged about thirteen or fourteen - off her hands to work on his farm "near the sea": an offer which she obviously accepted.

John grew up and acquired a farm of his own, his brother added, though it soon became apparent that he was not destined to stay in one place but rather to enjoy a life of adventure – whether by accident or design. Presumably because of his proximity to the sea, at about the same time John also acquired a sloop in which he proposed to carry coals from Whitehaven to sell in Ireland, an increasingly profitable and popular enterprise during the second half of the eighteenth century. Unfortunately, the boat sank in bad weather off the Cumberland coast and, whether John was on board and was rescued or whether he had simply invested in the venture and leased his boat to others, he lost the money he had put into the enterprise, forcing him to give up his farm and rejoin his family.

Robert junior is not specific on dates but says his family had by this time moved to Balmaclellan. He added that, as his father was also now in more regular contact with his family, and through the connections made during his travels, he was able to get John a position on another farm in Inch Parish, near Stranraer, in the far west of the region.

Paterson's wanderlust evidently ran strongly in his son, however, because shortly after this John took a passage on a ship called the *Golden Rule* bound for the American colonies, via Cork. This was apparently just before or at the outbreak of the American War of Independence, placing his departure in around 1775 or 1776, ie. when John was in his late twenties. Train, in his note to Scott enclosing Robert junior's letter, added that he thought John had left the region from Creetown *via* Whitehaven in 1774 which, given the context which follows, is equally plausible.[6]

Following his brother's departure, Robert junior said that there was little further correspondence between John and his family, despite the efforts of both Robert and Walter to write to him at an address where they understood he had settled, in Massachusetts, New England. The exception to this was a letter which Robert junior said his brother sent "not long" after his departure and which was apparently written while on his way to Hamburg, Germany. In that letter he described being held prisoner on a British man o' war.

There is no mention on Joseph Train's part of having seen or been given John's letter but, if he did, it has long since disappeared and we are left with only Robert junior's impression of a slightly confusing picture, written fifty years after the events described. The explanation, however, would appear to be that John had in fact become a sailor on a merchant vessel and that, prior to settling in America – if that is what he did – he enjoyed several years' voyaging about the shores of the north Atlantic and the Baltic seas, in the process becoming embroiled in the war with the American colonists.

The *Golden Rule* was a 'snow', derived from the Dutch 'snaw' or 'snauw' meaning 'beak', a reference to the pointed outline of the square-rigged, two-masted vessels which were typical of north European trading ships of the late eighteenth century. They were used for trade with America and the West Indies as well as in the Baltic and the Mediterranean. The snow had the advantage of being both large enough to carry a decent cargo and fast enough, in a good wind, to be used as a ship of preference by the Royal Navy. Indeed, when the navy needed additional ships in a hurry for one of the many continental wars of the period, they would frequently commandeer merchant snows which would then be fitted with a dozen or so guns and used for coastal defences or as privateers, raiding merchant vessels of other countries.

Built in Whitehaven in 1774, the *Golden Rule* could carry about 200 tons fully laden, around the average for trading vessels of the period.[7] Operating out of various ports on the west and south coasts of Britain, as well as Ireland, she began her trading life importing tobacco and cotton from Maryland and Virginia, then paid regular visits to the eastern Baltic ports, including St Petersburg, in Russia, and Memel, in modern Lithuania, from where she brought back timber. *En route* to or from America the ship would invariably stop over in Cork, while on the Baltic voyages she could call into Hamburg.*

Comparing the weekly reports of Lloyd's List of shipping and John's reported descriptions of his voyages and the incidents involved, it would appear that he served aboard the *Golden Rule* for at least some part, if not the whole, of the period between late 1775 and the autumn of 1780. In December 1775 the ship was reported as being "a transport", ie. that it been commandeered for use by the Royal Navy and it may be to this period that John alluded when he spoke about being "held prisoner" by a British man o'war. However, it is difficult to say as the location of the ship was not reported and when she returned it was to Cork and then Whitehaven, suggesting she had been operating somewhere in the north Atlantic .

It is more likely that the incident of which John wrote took place during a voyage home from the Baltic in late July 1780 when, according to Lloyd's List for 11th August, she was attacked by French privateers (France was an ally of the American colonists for most of the war). The *Golden Rule*, the report said,

> "... arrived the 3rd Inst. at Whitehaven, from Memel, much shattered in her sails and rigging by a French Privateer of 16 guns, off Cape Wrath, and would have been taken but for two ships, bound for Liverpool, who assisted her to escape."[8]

The assumption must be that the two ships that came to her assistance were British warships or else they would not have been able to deflect an attack from an armed enemy. Whatever damage was done to the ship must have been soon repaired, however, because the *Golden Rule* was reported to be berthed in Elsinore, Denmark, on 30 August and a month later had returned there from Memel, between which lies the port of Hamburg. It may therefore have been during this voyage that John wrote his letter to his family, reflecting on the close shave he had recently had and perhaps feeling just a little homesick.

The *Golden Rule* continued in merchant service for many more years to come and was finally reported as having been wrecked off the south coast of Ireland in August 1807, only some of its crew and cargo making it back to land. In the intervening years she made several more voyages to the Baltic, to the West Indies

---

* This summary of the voyages of the *Golden Rule,* and the itineraries which follow, are based on reports within the weekly Lloyd's List, 1774 to 1784 which have been digitised in www.maritimearchives.co.uk/lloyds-list.

– from where it would have brought back sugar and rum – and to north America, on one of which journeys John may have decided to jump ship to make a new life for himself.

Assuming John did eventually decide to settle in America, he became part of a small but increasing pattern of emigration of Scots during the eighteenth century, particularly from the southern lowlands where – as we shall see in the next chapter – agricultural improvements were pushing people off the land. It is estimated that a total of 80,000 Scots emigrated to what was to become the United States of America during the century: some 23,000 left between 1700-1760, all but 3,000 from the lowlands. However, 30,000 left from the lowlands alone between 1760 and 1775 and a further 5,000 once the War of Independence was over.[9]

Whatever the truth of the matter, little more was reported of John by his brother or by Joseph Train except for the curious 'Napoleon connection'. A *cause célèbre* around the turn of the eighteenth and nineteenth centuries had been the marriage of Jerome Bonaparte (a brother of Napoleon) to the daughter of an American merchant. In his letter to Train, Robert junior referred to the woman in question as Elizabeth Paterson (sic) and said he had long speculated on whether her father, a Baltimore merchant whose name, he thought, was John, might not be his long lost brother. A further coincidence, he noted, was that "Paterson of Baltimore" should name his son Robert, according to newspaper reports, and that he had also begun his career – he said - as a "privateer".[10]

Robert junior's comments were presented almost as an aside, for further reflection, at the end of his letter but Train was inevitably willing to jump to the obvious conclusions. "...(A)lthough you will see that what is stated in the enclosed communication", he told Scott in his covering letter, "does not amount to positive proof of the father of the wife of Napoleon's brother being the son of Old Mortality, I for my own part have no doubt that he was."[11] Scott, knowing when a story was too good to be true, forwarded Train's letter to his publishers with the advice that "the interesting information about the American Patersons be left out for the moment."[12]

The omission did not stop the story gaining currency and as late as 1870 local historians and correspondents to newspapers in Dumfriesshire reported the tale as fact.* The story was only able to be dismissed in 1873 when the Reverend Nathaniel Paterson, a great-grandson of Old Mortality who emigrated to Canada, was able to peruse the will of the Baltimore merchant who had died in 1827. He found that his name was in fact William Patterson and, while he had indeed

---

* See for example an article by Crawford Ramage, author of *Drumlanrig Castle and the Douglases,* in *Notes and Queries*, a Victorian magazine of eclectic tastes and contributions, of 10th September 1870. Ramage's contribution to the story is further addressed in Chapter Ten.

made his fortune in shipping around the time of the War of Independence and subsequently, he in fact came originally from Donegal, Ireland.[13] A few years later Elizabeth Bonaparte, near the end of her life and living in Paris, published her memoirs in which she confirmed the same.[14]

Francis

Back in Gatelawbridge, meanwhile, Paterson's brother Francis appears to have benefited from his absence to secure work on the rebuilding of Closeburn Manse. In 1763, according to the minutes of Penpont Presbytery (which covered both Morton and Closeburn Parishes), the local heritors were called together by Thomas Kirkpatrick of Closeburn to gain their views on what to do about the manse which was badly in need of repairs.[15]

Amongst their number was one Robert Alexander, described as a 'wright', which in this context appears to have meant a foreman or overseer of construction work. Alexander, and a colleague, John Duncan, "gave their opinion" that the manse and adjoining offices were in such a ruinous state that they needed to be rebuilt. They added, moreover, that they knew and could commission workmen for the job, such as "masons, wrights, glaziers and slaters" and named specifically Simon Porteous of Kirkbean as a slater and *Francis Paterson* of Applegarth as a mason.

Alexander and Duncan were therefore asked to go away and price up the costs of materials and labour required to do the job which, according to the Presbytery, they must have done as the minutes went on to record the estimate submitted. The mason's work, it was reported, would cost a surprisingly precise "£106, 5/2d and eight twelfths sterling" while the other work – including wrights, glaziers and slating - would cost a further £137 2/8d, making the total cost over £243, a not inconsiderable sum for the time.

In June 1763 the Presbytery session recorded that Sir Thomas had consequently "contracted with the said workmen" to rebuild the Manse, a task which would be finished by the following Martinmas, ie. November 1764. In fact the work seems to have been slightly delayed but was complete by 25 April 1765 when the heritors met again to inspect the workmanship. The minutes confirmed that Francis Paterson was the mason and that the standard of the finished work was considered to be "satisfactory in all respects".[16]

Aside from confirming the regional reputation which Francis had acquired as a stonemason, and therefore the trajectory of his own career, these references demonstrate the extent of the geographical area from which tradesmen could be sought for medium to large building projects at this period. They also back up the earlier suggestion that Robert Paterson would have travelled from Applegarth to work on the rebuilding of Closeburn Church in 1741.

It is ironic to think that the stone used on the rebuilding of the manse probably came from Gatelawbridge and that Paterson was no longer around to work with his brother once again or, indeed, to have won the commission in his stead. Given their previously good relationship, however, it would be pleasing to think that Francis was in contact with his sister-in-law during the time he worked on the manse and that he was able to provide some support to Elizabeth and her family in his brother's absence.

Balmaclellan
Robert Paterson did eventually return to his family, however. In 1768, according to Robert junior once again, his father "made us a visit, after an absence of ten years, brought us into Galloway, and took a house for us in the village of Balmaclellan".[17] Paterson senior, it seems, had developed enough of a base in the region to justify relocating his family to the heart of it. It is tempting to say that this was despite his wanderings but, as we saw in the previous chapter, there was a pattern and a focus to Paterson's whereabouts in this period which suggested that he had purposefully built up a network of contacts – both commercial and social – sufficient to consider that he and his family could have a rewarding life in Galloway.

Balmaclellan was then and still is a small village in the Ken Valley, about fifteen miles north of Castle Douglas and a couple of miles east of the river itself, and gave its name to the surrounding parish. The name comes from the Gaelic *Bail* meaning location, field or settlement, and 'MacClellan' from John of that surname who received his charter from James III in 1466 and whose family were responsible for the original development in the early middle ages. The site of a Norman motte, to the north of the church, was probably one of the family's original fortifications and dates from the late twelfth or early thirteenth centuries.

About half a mile north-east of this is Barscobe Castle, built in 1648 by William MacLellan and his wife Mary or Margaret Gordon - their initials and the date are inscribed in a stone above the door of the former ruin which has been more recently redeveloped as a private house. It was from Barscobe that their son Robert led a force of Covenanters to capture government soldiers in nearby Dalry in November 1666, so precipitating the Pentland Rising, mentioned in Chapter Six.

Mary or Margaret was the daughter of Sir Robert Gordon of Lochinvar, fourth Viscount Kenmure, the other major family of the area, upon one of whose ancestors Sir Walter Scott based the hero 'Young Lochinvar' in his epic poem *Marmion* (1808). The Gordons had held the title of Kenmure since 1633, when it was granted by Charles I, and had similarly secured the town charter for the development of New Galloway, in nearby Kells Parish. The town and the adjacent ruins of Kenmure Castle are both on the western shore of Loch Ken.

The Gordons were equally vociferous supporters of the Covenanting cause in the seventeenth century, though they later reverted to Catholicism and, indeed, made a habit of supporting the wrong side at various periods in history, as a result of which their fortunes had declined by the early years of the eighteenth century. They supported the Royalist cause during the Civil War, for which they were punished with the forfeiture of lands by Cromwell in the 1650s, and supported the Old Pretender, the Catholic James Stuart, during the 1715 rebellion, for which William Gordon, the sixth Viscount, paid with his life while more of his family's lands and titles were confiscated.

The area therefore had a strong Covenanting tradition led, unlike in Morton parish, by the local landowners, even if their fortunes had declined by the time that the Patersons moved there. In 1768 the resident heritors were John Gordon, the eighth Viscount Kenmure, and from another branch of the family, Alexander Spalding Gordon of Shirmers, the Deputy Sherif of Wigtown. The MacLellans had by this time concentrated their possessions and influence upon the town of Kirkcudbright, for which the impressive ruins of MacLellan Castle still stand testament.

Further reminders of the local Covenanting tradition could be found in the parish churchyard, in the centre of Balmaclellan, where there are several early eighteenth century headstones. These include the poorly inscribed grave of John Ierland (sic), a Covenanter who died in 1724, and a tablestone commemorating the Covenanter Robert Grierson, one of five men found at Ingliston Cave, near Moniaive in Glencairn parish, and subsequently shot by troops under the command of Colonel James Douglas on 28 April 1685. The parish church itself dates from 1753, though heavily altered in the nineteenth century, and would have been relatively new when the Patersons attended services there.

Just to the north of the village, reached by footpaths from Barscobe Castle, is Holy Linn waterfall, a local beauty spot in a bend of the Garple Burn which flows from here into the Ken. Similar to Crichope Linn in Morton Parish, in the seventeenth century the spot was renowned for the shelter which it afforded fugitive Covenanters while the 'outed' ministers of the parish baptised children in the river, just above Barscobe Loch.

Cheek by jowl with these – natural and man-made - monuments to Christian orthodoxy, and acting as a reminder of an equally violent age of superstition, was the hamlet and farm of Cubbox. About a mile south-west of Balmaclellan, it was the home of Elspeth MacEwan who was one of the last women to be tried as a witch in Scotland. In 1696, during a spell of poor harvests in the country as a whole, and amidst a population looking for scapegoats for the hardships they were suffering, she was accused of drawing milk from a neighbour's cows with a magical wooden pin and of preventing hens from laying eggs. McEwan was arrested and examined by members of Dalry Kirk session and then sent to Kirkcudbright for civil trial where, after nearly two years of imprisonment and torture, she was eventually found guilty of witchcraft, upon the evidence of witnesses, and burnt on a hill overlooking Kirkcudbright.

The local congregation, meanwhile, had a reputation for obstinacy and for upholding the morality of the church as strong as any parish in the region. While the records of the kirk session for the period have not survived, there exists a petition presented by one residing heritor, three elders of the kirk and forty-one heads of families plus fourteen other residents objecting to the moral suitability of the Reverend William McKie, who was called to be the minister of the parish in April 1746.

The petition cited *Fama Clamosa* or an objection on the grounds that there were rumours ascribing immoral conduct to the minister. The objections were probably genuine as the involvement of the local heritors suggests that it was not a case of 'patronage', but they were not upheld by the Presbytery and McKie went on to become minister in June 1747, remaining so until 1763 when his son took over. Nathaniel McKie was the minister when the Patersons arrived in the parish.

Elizabeth (2)
By the time the Patersons came to live in Balmaclellan, it had a population of around 500 people, of whom perhaps seventy or eighty lived in the village itself. These figures are estimates, based on a combination of 'Webster's Census of 1755' and the more detailed report contained in the Old Statistical Account for the parish in 1792, between which the population hardly changed. The former was a census of just over 900 parishes in Scotland, coordinated by Alexander Webster, an Edinburgh minister, in 1755,[18] while the latter was undertaken by the Reverend James Thomson, the local minister and author of the account.[19]

We can be fairly precise about where the Patersons lived in Balmaclellan because of information from a number of sources. The first is the Reverend Thomson's census, which was apparently undertaken in one night in February 1792, and contains an entry for "no.9 Balmaclellan Causey" in which lived "Robert Paterson 33, Margaret Paterson 40, Janet Landers 4, and Thomas Landers (no age given)".[20] "Causey" referred to a 'causeway' or main, usually cobbled, street within a small town or village which suggests that the address was in the centre of Balmaclellan.

Allowing for some discrepancies in their ages (perhaps including some guesswork or gallantry by the minister in the case of his parishioners), "Robert Paterson" was Robert junior, unmarried, still living in the family home and actually thirty-five years old; while "Margaret Paterson" was Paterson senior's eldest daughter, by then in reality forty-seven years old.

Parish registers for Balmaclellan for the period concerned were kept but, as the minister himself commented in the Statistical Account, individual entries were scarce due to the fees imposed by the state for the registration of births, deaths and marriages. This makes it difficult to establish with precision some of the more significant dates in the Patersons' lives. However, we can establish, by cross-referencing the events and dates that *are* recorded, that Margaret married Thomas Landers, probably in 1773, and that they had at least two children: Elizabeth, in 1774, and Thomas, in 1776. The "Thomas Landers" living with her in 1792 was therefore either her husband, whose age we don't know, or her son, by then about fifteen years of age. Janet Landers, finally, may have been their latest child.

The second source for the family's location came from Mrs Janet Clement McLellan, the eighty-three year old whose description of seeing Old Mortality when she was a child we read in the last chapter. Mrs McLellan's childhood home, she remembered, was the site of what by 1870 was the local post office and which remains a general store and rural post office to this day. The Patersons, she said, lived across the road, which placed their home in the very centre of the village.

The third source is traditional but ironically even more precise and relates to the employment which Elizabeth found for herself once she had settled in the village. According to Joseph Train, Elizabeth ran "a little school" in Balmaclellan and used the "small pittance" derived from this to support her family while her husband continued on his travels.[21] He did not specify its location but local tradition has it that "Mrs Paterson's Adventure School" was in the centre of the village, "up the lane directly opposite the shop and on the left after a lamp post."[22] It was apparently housed in an outbuilding attached to the family home and the cottage in question still stands, albeit semi-derelict, having been used in more recent years as a garage/engineering workshop.

We know from the minutes of the parish heritors' meetings that Balmaclellan did not have a formal school building until 1785 and, as we saw in the last chapter, that the commission for its building went to Walter Paterson. Up until that point, apparently, the children of the parish were taught within the church, a traditional venue for rural areas at the time. William Smith was the teacher from at least 1782 but it is not clear when he started his duties and it would appear that, for a few years during the 1770s at least, Elizabeth Paterson either provided this facility herself or ran a school in competition to the one established by the parish.

These private or 'adventure' schools were quite common in rural areas at the time and were established by enterprising local residents or sometimes just by local parents desperate to improve on parish provision. By their nature, they were usually inferior to parish schools, having poorly or non-qualified teachers, offering a very basic range of subjects and, in many cases, operating in worse physical conditions, but their proliferation was an indication of the desire (at least by parents) for education. Although the authorities had a vested interest in avoiding competition for the parish schools, they rarely tried to shut down private schools in recognition of the role they played. According to TC Smout in his *History of the Scottish People* (1969),

> "Between them, the parochial schools and the adventure schools of the Lowlands were able to maintain a rural society in which almost everyone seems to have been able to read and write from at least as early as the mid-eighteenth century... That was a remarkable achievement, certainly not paralleled in England, and probably not paralleled in many societies anywhere in the world." [23]

The fees which Elizabeth would have been able to command for teaching the children of local residents were little changed from those which Paterson's father was paying in Hawick towards the beginning of the century, and were little different twenty-five years later, as confirmed in the reports from many parishes in the Old Statistical Account. Fees at adventure schools were in line with these even though the teachers concerned were not entitled to an additional salary from the heritors. This suggests that Elizabeth might have received around 1/6d a quarter (ie. per term) per child for teaching reading and writing. A premium of 2/- a quarter could be charged for Latin and arithmetic but it is not clear whether her own education ran to this standard of teaching.

The new school building in Balmaclellan was built with the benefit of an endowment of £500 sterling recently left by a Mr Murdoch, a retired Glasgow merchant, which the heritors had invested in land and which was yielding about five per cent or £25 a year[24]: almost enough to fund the capital costs of the school and sufficient to sustain its running well into the future without touching the original sum. The heritors were therefore able to guarantee the schoolteacher the legal maximum state salary (by 1785) of about £11; but a condition of the endowment was that he could receive no other wages, ie. that he could not charge the children anything for attending school. This meant that parents had no incentive to send their children anywhere else and effectively put a stop to any local competition.

Even if she had still been teaching in 1785, it is therefore likely that Elizabeth would have lost her source of employment. As it was, and quite ironically, Elizabeth died on 5 May 1785, aged fifty-nine, two months before the new school was completed.

The Remaining Family

In February 1830, while he was still compiling information for the revised edition of *Old Mortality*, Sir Walter Scott received a letter from one "J G Barbour of Borgue", near Kirkcudbright. The letter supplemented information already supplied by Train regarding Paterson's family and provided further details of his grandchildren, some of whom went on to have distinguished careers in the church, in commerce and in academia, ending up in the north of England, the United States of America, Canada, Russia and New Zealand.

Barbour claimed "lineal and lateral descent from the biographer of Bruce" and claimed also to have met Joseph Train although "his visit might be cursory". Getting to the point, he had a knowledge of Old Mortality's family, he said, which stemmed from living "within a mile" of Balmaclellan for the previous thirty years of his life. "Indeed," he continued,

> "I may claim a nipple kindred (if I may use such a homely expression) with the very family of Old Mortality, I having been suckled by Margaret Paterson, his daughter, when my own mother through illness was unable to supply the first aliment of nature."[25]

We have already seen that Margaret settled down in Balmaclellan with a husband and family of her own. Of Janet, unfortunately, we have little further information.

Regarding Paterson's remaining sons, however, there is more evidence, derived from Barbour, parish registers and the family headstones, which stand together in Balmaclellan churchyard. According to these sources, Walter Paterson, Elizabeth's second oldest son, married Mary Locke. The date is not known but was possibly in early 1785, just prior to Elizabeth's passing, as their first recorded child was christened on 5 November that year and named - Elizabeth. They later had two sons, Walter and Nathaniel, both of whom became ministers. Walter senior later acquired the tenancy of Holm Farm, about half a mile north-west of Balmaclellan where he died on 9 May 1812, aged sixty-three.

Nathaniel Paterson, already referred to in connection with the story of John Paterson, was the minister for Galashiels, in the Borders, overlapping with Sir Walter Scott's residence at nearby Abbotsford to which, interestingly, he became a frequent visitor. Remarks later made by Scott show that he knew the connection and it would be fascinating to know what discussions they had on the occasions of Paterson's visits to the novelist but, according to his biographer he showed little interest in his family background. Of the possible 'Napoleon connection', for example, Anderson says that Nathaniel Paterson "knew nothing more than is generally known and never deemed the matter worth investigation."[26]

Robert Paterson junior went on to marry Agnes McNaught (this is according to the parish register; their family headstone says McKnight) in Balmaclellan on 29 January 1795. They had at least four children as follows:

- Alexander, on 10 October 1795;
- John, on 26 December 1796; and
- Robert, on 12 May 1799.

The fourth son, Thomas, presumably born after 1799, was still alive in 1855 when he had the family tombstone erected.

Robert Paterson junior died on 30 April 1846 and was a shoemaker. His wife, Agnes, died in August 1818.

Notes

1   Ramage, CT, *op cit.*
2   Rev James Smaill, OSA, Parish of Dornock, Dumfriesshire, 1790
3   David Loch, *A Tour through most of the Trading Towns and Villages of Scotland*, 1788.
4   *Ibid*
5   Paterson, Robert Jnr, letter to Joseph Train, 9 May 1829, National Library of Scotland, MS874
6   Train to Scott, Letter of 12 May 1829 enclosing the above, NLS, MS874
7   Lloyd's Register of Shipping, 1776
8   Lloyd's List, 11 July 1780.
9   Tyson, Robert E, 'Demographic Change', chapter 12 of *Eighteenth Century Scotland – New Perspectives*, Ed. TM Devine & JR Young, 1993
10 Paterson, Robert Jnr, 9 May 1829, *op cit*
11 Joseph Train to Sir Walter Scott, 12 May 1829, *op cit.*
12 *Letters of Sir Walter Scott* Vol.XI, 1828-31, ed. HJC Grierson
13 Anderson, Alexander, preface and memoir in *Letters To His Family*, Nathaniel Paterson, 1874. This Nathaniel Paterson was *Old Mortality's* grandson – it was his son, Nathaniel junior, who emigrated.
14 Didier, EL, *The Life & Letters of Madame Bonaparte*, London 1879.
15 Penpont Presbytery, 1756-67 (National Library of Scotland, CH2/298/6)
16 *Ibid*
17 Ramage, CT, *op cit.*
18 Alexander Webster, *An account of the number of people in Scotland in the year seventeen hundred and fifty-five*. A copy of a transcription of the account, made by James Gray Kyd and published in 1952, is available on the website of the National Records of Scotland.
19 Thomson, Rev. James, OSA, Stewartry of Kirkcudbright, Balmaclellan Parish, 1792.
20 Entry no.108 in the census contained within the above account.
21 Joseph Train to Sir Walter Scott, 31 March 1829, *op cit*
22 Campbell, Anna, *Glenkens Schools*, 2002
23 Smout, TC, *A History of the Scottish People 1560-1830*, Collins 1969
24 Heritors' minutes for Balmaclellan 1782-95
25 *Letters to Scott, 1826-32*, National Library of Scotland, 1834 (MS 869). Barbour, like Joseph Train, with whom he was acquainted, was a local historian and antiquarian.
26 Anderson, Alexander, *op cit.*

CHAPTER NINE

HIS DEATH

Changing Times
In his *Chiselprints of Old Mortality*, James King Hewison provided a description of Paterson in his later years based on an amalgam of contemporary sources. We have seen how he maintained a commercial aspect to his career, despite his itinerant lifestyle, and that this was not unusual in the context of the rural society of the late eighteenth century. But the portrait painted was of a medieval wanderer rather than of a modern tradesman. He was remembered, Hewison said:

> "as a little, bent, wizened old body of four score years and weird to look upon. Beneath his once blue Kilmarnock bonnet straggled bunches of long white hair, over shrunken, rounded shoulders. His clothes of shepherd's hoddin were waulked and 'scaured' by storm and sun, which did not add beauty to those baggy productions, ill shapen by some Galloway 'whip-the-cat'." *[1]

It is clear that Paterson's appearance and outlook, as much as the views of the strict Covenanting populations with whom he felt at home, were by the end of the eighteenth century becoming increasingly anachronistic.

A number of changes had taken place in the countryside through which Paterson travelled in the last forty years of the century, and they were to a great extent inter-related. The main factors at play were an increase in population, and in its urbanisation, the beginnings of industrialisation and improvements in agriculture, together with the advances in transport infrastructure described in Chapter Seven. These in turn stemmed from greater political stability, since the defeat of Jacobite forces in 1746, and enhanced trade, especially with neighbouring England.

During the second half of the century, while the population of Scotland as a whole increased by over a quarter, the urban population expanded by much more. Towns and villages of over 2,000 people, which represented one in ten of the population in 1750, had by 1800 come to contain one in three people.[2] The trend was intensified in the south-west of Scotland which saw an overall increase in population of more than a third between 1755-1801, while individual parishes – notably those with emerging urban centres - saw greater expansion still. The population of Nithsdale, for example, grew by over forty per cent and, within this, the population of Morton parish almost tripled in size (albeit from a very low base), due mainly to the expansion of Thornhill.[3]

---

* The contemporary name given to travelling tailors.

The rising population was largely accounted for by:

- the elimination of smallpox: inoculation had begun in 1721 and had become much more prevalent as the century progressed. Together with changes in child-rearing practices generally, these factors led to overall increases in birth and survival rates with life expectancy increasing by six years between 1755 and the 1790s;[4]
- improvements in diet: potatoes had become ubiquitous by the 1790s, featuring as part of perhaps seventy-five to eighty per cent of meals compared to their virtual non-existence in the 1740s;[5] and
- increasing prosperity: resulting from the greater prevalence of jobs in traditional and new industries, improvements in agriculture and the rise in incomes associated with both.

Increases in the population of individual parishes could be accounted for by local developments such as coal and mineral mining, quarrying and new industries such as textile weaving but also iron-making, sugar boiling, building and woollens. Closeburn, in Nithsdale, with its increasing reliance on limestone quarrying and the consequent improvement in soils and harvests, saw a sixty-eight per cent increase in its population over the same period.

Further west, the customs port of Kirkcudbright, serving fifty miles of the local coastline, saw a fifty per cent increase in population to 2,300 by 1792. Girthon parish, including the newly industrialised town of Gatehouse, grew by sixty per cent on the basis of cotton spinning and had 1150 inhabitants, many also employed in the tannery and soap works. And there were many other such examples.

That said, industry in Scotland, and especially in Dumfriesshire and Galloway, was still small-scale and widely scattered. Even by the turn of the century, with one third of the population in urban centres, that left two-thirds still living in the countryside. And here, in the remoter, rural parishes, the concomitant issue over the period in question was a *decrease* in population.

This was because of a lack of local industry and consequent emigration to the towns, but was also due to a trend towards the amalgamation of farm holdings which required fewer people to be on the land in any case. That trend was due, in turn, to the exploitation of advances in both arable and pastoral practices, for example in soil improvements and crop rotation in the lowlands and enhanced grass yields and species selection for cattle and sheep rearing in the hills.

The census undertaken by the Reverend James Thomson in Balmaclellan in 1792, for example, suggested that, if anything, the local population had probably fallen slightly since Webster's Census of 1755 (see Chapter Eight). Although neither census can be regarded as completely accurate, the numbers are significant in the context of the increasing size of towns just a few miles away, along the region's coastline. The earlier census recorded a population of 534 while the later one suggested this had declined to around 495, comprising "231 males and 264 females", of whom 77 lived in the village itself.[6] This fall, Thomson suggested, could be attributed to changes in agricultural practices, including improvements in soil resulting from the use of lime from Closeburn, which were yielding better crops with fewer labourers on the land.

The upshot was an acceleration in the adoption and prevalence of more commercial farming practices such as those we previously saw coming to the fore on larger estates, forcing tenants to farm for the market rather than for themselves or their relations and neighbours. By 1750, for example, only about five per cent of estates in the south-west of Scotland were involved in the enclosure of property to consolidate grazing land: the trend had been slowed by opposition to over-enthusiastic adoption of the practice by landowners in the Ken Valley and around Wigtown in the 1720s, as we saw in Chapter Six. However, by the 1780s this had risen to nearly two-thirds of estates. And by the 1790s, it had become normal for farm leases to prescribe specific cropping practices to be followed as conditions of tenancy.[7]

In both industry and agriculture, therefore, massive investment was taking place in the expectation of equally large returns. In his *History of the Scottish People*, TC Smout noted that a turning point in the relations of tenant farmers with their landlords, and in their respective attitudes to enterprise, was reached with the sale of the medieval estate of Baldoon, near Wigtown in Galloway in 1787. The new owners subsequently auctioned off the land in parcels to the highest bidders and the high prices which were achieved astounded local farmers.[8] As one nineteenth century commentator remarked:

> "... when the lands of Baldoon fell by purchase into the possession of the house of Galloway... rents were offered that never had been dreamed of by a Galloway farmer. Farm rents had in the course of ages crept up from a few pounds a year to a few hundreds, but on that occasion farms of moderate extent were let at above two thousand a year."[9]

Similarly, in the parish of Troqueer, just to the west of Dumfries, an estate which fetched £950 in 1760 commanded £4750 by 1790.[10] For all those involved, Smout commented, a new era had been entered.

These trends led to increases in prices but also in net incomes as the population was not rising as fast as productivity. For those who managed to stay on the land or to find gainful employment elsewhere, rents climbed and the price of some staple foods rose slightly through the turn of eighteenth and nineteenth centuries, but the average wage rose still further. As an example, a ploughman earning £2 or £3 in the 1750s saw his wage more than double by the last decade of the century to about £7 a year in cash and about the same again in kind if he were married.[11] By contrast, in rural parishes like Balmaclellan, the Reverend Thomson reported that the average rent was still an affordable 2/6d an acre.

By this time people living in the country had also begun to grow a more varied assortment of fruit and vegetables in their own gardens, including turnips, carrots and potatoes along with currants, gooseberries and mint. Meat was also more weekly or bi-weekly fare rather than being saved for special occasions.[12] This variety also meant that families could be 'buffered' against hard times, or even famine, were one crop to fail. In addition, it meant that they could take surpluses to market and earn a little more income.

A New Landscape

The Old Statistical Account, describing social and economic conditions in each parish of the country during the early 1790s, provided the first comprehensive and detailed report on life in the region. In doing so, the local ministers who usually produced the reports painted a picture in words which largely supported the statistics already given – and they saw that it was good.

They referred to increases in agricultural productivity, the emergence of specific local industries, the development of new towns and villages or the construction of new houses (and the houses being roofed in slate), as well as new roads and bridges. Reporting on social conditions, they nearly always remarked on the rise in the local population, especially of urban areas, as well as increases in incomes, and in many cases talked about improvements in social conditions and diets.[13]

Comparisons were inevitably drawn between life as it had been in the middle of the century, and as it had become by the period of writing and, generally speaking, the reporters in most parishes agreed that life had greatly improved. They tended less often to talk about changes for the worse or how they affected the outlook and behaviour of local residents.

Robert Paterson would have been in a perfect position to view these changes for himself by virtue of his extensive travels through the region over the whole of the period concerned. For him, as for anyone living at the time, the changes would of course have been gradual and, despite the apparent general progress, there would have remained even by the 1790s large areas of more remote countryside where conditions were little changed: with few new industries, traditional systems of agriculture still in place and roads which were still poor.

But changes were afoot: some quite visible, such as the development of new towns, as at Gatehouse, and the expansion of others, together with their new houses and industrial buildings and the increase in their resident populations.

They would have looked and felt more crowded. The physical landscape of the countryside was changing as well, at least in the valley bottoms and along the coast, from scattered 'farmtoun' communities with their shared open fields and common land, to individual farms with walled crops and sheep and cattle enclosures.

Other changes were more subtle. Towns and villages were increasing in size in part through organic growth but also due to the immigration of people who no longer had work, or even a place to live, in the countryside. In rural areas, meanwhile, the pressure to be more efficient was forcing tenant farmers to be more competitive and to work for themselves and their immediate families rather than their traditional communities. In both cases, a new generation of Scots was being forced to earn money in order to make a living, as opposed to living off their own produce, however inefficiently, and perhaps selling the little that was left over. This undermined the cooperative basis of traditional communities and the sense of communion that ran through them and which was the foundation of their social life.

More insidiously, particularly in the larger towns, a generation was growing up whose focus was increasingly on work to make ends meet, rather than worrying about the loss of social ideals. Within this population a new, educated middle class was also developing whose emphasis was on property, comfort and ensuring an adequate income for their families. Their values were those of the Enlightenment: defending the state, the importance of the market economy and a rational approach to religion.

While none of this was controversial, it left people with little time or inclination to fret about the nature of God or to interpret the Bible for moral guidance and still less to commemorate the fanaticism of some of their ancestors. Scotland was still a God-fearing nation where the great majority of people attended church, but decreasingly few were prepared to "make a continual trade of religion", as Ralph Erskine, one of the leading Covenanter preachers of the mid-eighteenth century had argued. This pattern was confirmed by the observations of a number of ministers in the Old Statistical Account, for example the Reverend Muter who wrote of his parishioners in 1792:

> "The people of Kirkcudbright are, in general, of a pleasant, social and agreeable disposition, and their morals are fully as good as those of their neighbours... Their reading is extensive... and they have access to all the improvements in literature and politics. They are all loyal to government... and averse to divisions in the Church. No minister in the Church of Scotland can boast of such unanimity amongst his people: for among the whole 2,295 that compose the parish, there is not one dissenter, or seceder, of any denomination, whatever."[14]

In practical terms, this meant that the population of like minds with whom Paterson could spend time was rapidly diminishing, reducing his choice of rural homes with sympathetic families in which to stay - and possibly accounting for his need to stay in commercial lodgings by the end of his life.

A Pauper's Funeral

It was in this context that Paterson was to be found, at the age of eighty-four, still looking to buy headstones from quarries near Dumfries during the winter of 1800/01. According to his son Robert junior, he had first gone to Locharbriggs Quarry, a site on the northern fringes of the town which is still worked today. "After stopping there five or six days," he said, "and all that time complaining of a pain in his bowels, he set out for Bankend, in the parish of Caerlaverock".[15]

Caerlaverock parish occupies the east coast of the Nith estuary, to the south of Dumfries, where it runs between muddy banks draining mile after mile of flat salt marshes into the Solway. The mud and marshland are evidence of millennia of human failure to fight back a gradual silting of the estuary, ever since the Romans built a harbour to service their occupation of southern Scotland in the second century AD, overlooked, as the parish name suggests, by a fort on the copse-covered hill of Ward Law. The site of the former port is now a mile from the sea.

Robert junior hypothesised that his father had gone to Bankend because of the presence there of a small freestone quarry and because of its proximity to the port of Glencaple, on the Nith Estuary, from where the headstones he acquired could be carried by boat closer to their destination, which he assumed to be Wigtownshire. At this time Glencaple was one of the ports of Dumfries and a thriving centre for shipbuilding. By the 1790s the ships calling or leaving from here, though rarely of ocean-going size, averaged about fifty or sixty ton cargos with some carrying up to ninety tons. (Larger ships called at Carsethorne, six miles further south on the opposite coast.) They brought lime and coal from Cumberland and foodstuffs from Liverpool and took away potatoes and grain.[16]

Given the relatively short biography which Robert junior provided of his father, the account of his death is quite detailed. Compared with earlier events which happened before he was born or while he was still a child and which are related in summary form, the final scene bears all the hallmarks of a first hand account which Robert junior may have been given in person. "He was got", Robert said, "within a very short distance of the house of Bankend", which other commentators have interpreted as the quarrymaster's house, "where some persons at the door observed him approaching, apparently in an uneasy posture, or some rather strange appearance about him."

Paterson was apparently riding on his horse or pony, which suggests that he had still to purchase or carve for himself a headstone to take away. "While they were looking at him," Robert junior continued, "he fell from the horse." The locals then ran to Paterson's aid, "the white pony standing beside him", lifted him up and carried him into the house where he was resuscitated, albeit briefly. Paterson, his son added, "was able to speak, and told who he was, and where his sons lived." Then, in a poignant last line which harks back to the discussion of Paterson's birth date in Chapter Two and sums up how little his family knew of him, he wrote:

"He was born in 17(12?), died on the 29th January 1801."[17]

Whether or not Robert junior or other members of his family were able to attend the subsequent funeral is unclear. His letter to Train implies that the authorities knew where to send for the old man's next of kin and Train himself confirmed that "as soon as his body was found, intimation was sent to his sons at Balmaclellan". However, Train added, "the great depth of the snow at that time" prevented the news reaching his family in time for them to attend their father's burial.

There are doubts about the accuracy of Train's version of events, for reasons which will become apparent later. But it does seem from the list of funeral expenses which Robert junior passed to Joseph Train, and which Train transcribed for Sir Walter Scott, that Paterson was given a pauper's funeral, provided by the local kirk. This suggests that the family was not present to oversee and pay for arrangements themselves or, indeed, to take the body back to Balmaclellan. The list is the second document given to Train but, like the accompanying letter and list of lodging expenses discussed in Chapter Seven, the original has disappeared. However, as reproduced by Train and as subsequently printed in the introduction to the 1830 edition of *Old Mortality*, it read:

"To a coffin,	£ 0 12	0
To munting (making) for d(itt)o.	0 2	8
To a shirt for him,	0 5	6
To a pair of Cotten Stockings,	0 2	0
To bread at the founral,	0 2	6
To Chise at ditto.	0 3	0
To 1 pint Rume,	0 4	6
To 1 pint Whiskie,	0 4	0
To a man going to Annan,	0 2	0
To the grave digger,	0 1	0
To linnen for a sheet for him,	0 2	8
	L 2 1	10
Taken off him when dead,	1 7	6
	L 0 14	4"[18]

Included in the transcription but omitted by Scott from the text of his novel was a postscript in which Robert junior testified to the authenticity of the note:

"That the above is a correct account of the funeral charges of Robert Paterson my father who went under the name of Old Mortality, which account has been in my possession from the time of his death was given by me this day to Mr Joseph Train, Supervisor of the Excise Castle Douglas, is attested by me
(signed) Robert Paterson,
Balmaclellan Village, 20 September 1827
Witnesses to the signature of Robert Paterson Son of Old Mortality
R Bell (James?) Farmer (Hardhic?)
John Finlay Distiller Bank".[19]

Further corroboration of the nature of Paterson's burial was provided a few years later in a notebook kept by Dr Thomas Boyle Grierson of Thornhill (1818-89), a local antiquarian who later set up a museum in the town. Grierson, like many of his contemporaries in the same field of enquiries, was notoriously lax in his fact-checking and his notebook is filled with conjectures and contradictions. His notes concerning Old Mortality, for example, written in 1857, referred to Paterson and his family living at once in Newton and on the site of the (recently built) poorhouse, which was in Gatelawbridge.

On the same page, however, Grierson recorded a conversation he had had with a local stonecutter, Robert Hastings, who had been commissioned to engrave the Paterson family headstone erected in Balmaclellan in 1855. The notes included a transcription of a version of the funeral expenses set out above, which Grierson says he "had from Robert Hastings" while acknowledging that the original came from Joseph Train. Crucially, he added that, according to the same source, he believed that Paterson "died with (ie. was buried with) William Stewart", a practice which was not unknown in pauper funerals.[20]

The parishioners of Caerlaverock also appear to have provided Paterson with a fresh shirt (most probably fashioned like a nightgown) and stockings, not surprising given the likely condition of the clothes in which he arrived, and to have wrapped him in a linen sheet prior to burial. In view of the weather, it is very possible that the body – or bodies – would then have been left outside in the cold awaiting burial, possibly for up to two weeks. A further distinguishing feature of pauper funerals is that the deceased were buried in unmarked graves.

Regarding the funeral expenses, two things stand out to the casual observer. The first is that the costs involved seem quite expensive relative to contemporary prices, suggesting that the local kirk session made a healthy profit on the event, at least ensuring that they could justify holding onto the money found in Paterson's

---

* It is difficult to read the handwriting in Train's manuscript at this point, hence the words in parentheses and question marks.

belongings. The second, probably not unrelated to the first, is that some of the items bought for the burial, notably the amount of alcohol included, sit oddly with the notion of a 'pauper's funeral'. This apparent contradiction must have struck Scott as well because a month after supplying the above details, Train wrote again with evidence to illustrate the 'excesses' which were often involved in funerals among the rural poor, despite their lack of income.

"A vain display of pomp and family pride at Funerals", wrote Train, referring to practices which had only recently died out, "then extended down to the peasantry in such a degree that the person who had arrived at the age of thirty years without having set apart from his earnings, however scanty his income might be, a sum sufficient to defray the expenses of a Funeral in a style becoming his rank in society was accounted very improvident indeed."[21]

Train then went on to relate the example of a 'Cameronian' funeral which had taken place in Rerrick parish, east of Kirkcudbright, as recently as 1823. The deceased, a local farmer, had apparently saved enough money to pay for a service, prior to his burial, to which over a hundred people were invited. The service, held in a meeting house in Castle Douglas, involved a blessing by the local minister after which successive rounds of food and drink were circulated.

The first round, according to Train, who said his report was based on evidence provided by "Mr William Young spirit dealer Castle Douglas", "consisted of Whisky and shortbread... the second of Brown Stout and Edinburgh Ale...with Buns and Cheese. The third of Port and plum cakes..." and so on, continuing in similar fashion for seven rounds in total before the congregation somehow travelled to Dundrennan for the burial, after which further refreshments were taken in the village schoolhouse.[22] While Paterson's own funeral service was obviously not so lavish, it would therefore appear that the parishioners of Caerlaverock – who, after all, Paterson may have known through previous visits to the local quarry – decided to make use of his 'savings' to ensure he had a decent send-off.

A Final Resting Place?
Interesting and darkly comic though Train's accounts might be, he did a considerable disservice to the subject of his story, and to posterity, by confusing both the date and more crucially the location of Paterson's death and subsequent burial – the latter possibly deliberately. His reasons for doing so are not entirely clear, but his actions prevented the site from being formally identified, and Old Mortality's memory commemorated, until much later in the nineteenth century.

As we have seen, Paterson's grave was not marked. Traditionally, as a pauper's grave, it would have been one of several indistinguishable plots dug on the shaded, north side of the former church site, away from the sunnier aspects favoured by those who could afford formal funeral services and headstones. Compounding this was the fact that records of deaths were either not kept in Caerlaverock at this time or have been lost – the funeral service was not one of the sacraments of the church and, even where formal records of births, deaths and marriages were kept, burials were the least likely to be registered. There was also no legal requirement to do so until the middle of the new century.

Thus we have to take the word of Robert junior for the facts relating to his father's death and subsequent burial. Although he does not appear to have attended the actual funeral, the amount of detail contained in his letter, and the fact that he acquired the list of funeral expenses, would suggest that he did eventually travel to Bankend and was able to talk to local people who had observed the events at first hand and had possibly even attended the internment (although the amount of alcohol consumed might have contributed to some blurred memories). Certainly, he did not make an issue of this in his own letter.

In contrast, Joseph Train's account of Paterson's death contained none of the detail provided by Robert junior in his letter, aside from the list of funeral expenses. In his letter to Scott Train simply says that Paterson "died, *as you have described* (my emphasis), at Bankhill, near Lockerby, on the 14th of February, 1801", ie. some twenty miles from Bankend and sixteen days after the date given by his son.[23]

Dealing with the date first, this may have resulted from genuine confusion over the date of Paterson's death as opposed to his burial which, as we have seen, could have been severely delayed by the weather and the anticipated arrival of his family. The difference in locations, however, was not a slip of the pen - Train referred to Bankhill four times in total in his text, including an explicit insertion in the heading for the funeral expenses. Referring to Robert junior he added, "My friend was prevented by indisposition from even going to Bankhill to attend the funeral of his father, which I regret very much, as he is not aware in what churchyard he was interred."[24]

These statements not only conflict with Robert junior's version of events but the last also contradicts Train's earlier assertion that Paterson's relations had actually – albeit belatedly – reached Bankhill (or Bankend). It may also be worth noting that, in the only other known transcription of the list – albeit one that is also secondhand - Thomas Grierson of Thornhill cites the location as "Bankend of Caerlaverock" and the date as "14 Feby". The same information is inscribed on the family memorial to Paterson in Balmaclellan churchyard and all three sources refer to him being eighty-eight when he died (and therefore born in 1712), suggesting that everyone was taking their information from the list of funeral expenses, with only Train departing from the text with regard to the location.

Without access to records or the original list of funeral expenses it is difficult to make assertions but if Train did deliberately alter a key fact relating to Paterson's death, what could his motives possibly have been? The only one which suggests itself, as we have seen in earlier chapters, is that Train may not have wanted to lose face by admitting to Scott that the thrust - in the case of his 'Cameronian' tendencies - and some of the key facts - in the case of his death - of Paterson's life, as he had first related them, were untrue.

The subtleties of the development of Paterson's Covenanting principles were discussed in Chapter Six. With regard to the details of Paterson's death we are on shakier ground as Train began his letter of 31 March 1829 by confessing that Paterson was not born in Closeburn, as he had originally thought, but "merely moved there while still relatively young". However, Paterson's place of birth was not mentioned in previous texts of the novel, whereas the area in which he died explicitly was – based, presumably, on facts originally given by Train in 1816. The need to maintain this version of events may have added to the list of reasons why Train chose to transcribe the letter from Paterson junior, and the documents he had been given, rather than sending them directly to Scott. By contrast, and as we saw in the last chapter, he *was* able to enclose the original of a second letter, received in May, as it concerned Paterson's son John and other matters which were not previously discussed in the novel.

Whatever the real reasons for these discrepancies, the fact remained that, ironically for a man who spent his life recording the final resting places of so many others, both the date of Paterson's death and the precise location in which he was buried were cast in doubt. In his response to Train of 18 April 1829, Scott lamented this fact and added "I would certainly erect a monument to his memory at my own expense."[25] True to his word, Scott left sufficient monies in his will to cover the expense of erecting a memorial and instructions to his publishers to attempt to locate Paterson's grave site in order to do so.

Little, if anything, appears to have been done about this by the original publishers of Scott's novels but in 1851 the copyright was bought by Adam and Charles Black. Such was the enduring popularity of his works, and of *Old Mortality* in particular, that research into the details of Paterson's death was eventually undertaken by David Laing (1793-1878), Secretary of the Scottish Society of Antiquaries, who had a particular interest in matters concerning the Covenanters. Laing gave his opinion, based on sources already cited above but also on correspondence with Nathaniel Paterson, one of Walter Paterson's sons, that the patriarch had indeed died at Bankend, not Bankhill, and that he was interred in the churchyard of Caerlaverock.[26]

The publishers consequently commissioned a headstone which was erected in Bankend of Caerlaverock churchyard in 1869, though not on the actual grave which was never established. The issue of the date of Paterson's death was also fudged by the use of the words "buried here, February 1801". It was inscribed:

"Erected to the memory of Robert Paterson.
The *Old Mortality* of Sir Walter Scott,"

and concludes with lines from *The Wallflower*, by the Reverend John Langhorne (1735-79), which introduce Chapter One of the novel, ie.:

"Why seeks he with unwearied toil
Through death's dim walks to urge his way,
Reclaim his long asserted spoil,
and lead oblivion into day?"[27]

Notes

1   Hewison, JK, *Chisel Prints...*, op cit
2   *Eighteenth Century Scotland – New Perspectives*, Ed. TM Devine & JR Young, 2003
3   Campbell, RH, 'The Population of SW Scotland from the mid-18th century to 1911', *Transactions* III, Vol.60, p82 (1985)
4   Devine & Young, 2003, *op cit*
5   MacRobert, AE, 'The Statistical Accounts', in *Transactions* III, Vol.82, p83 (2008)
6   Thomson, Rev James, OSA, Stewartry of Kirkcudbright, Balmaclellan Parish, 1792, *op cit.*
7   Devine, TM, *The Transformation Of Rural Scotland: Social Change And The Agrarian Economy 1660-1815*, 1999.
8   Smout, TC, *A History Of The Scottish People 1560-1830*, Collins 1969.
9   Robinson, Samuel, *Reminiscences of Wigtownshire about the close of the last century, 1872*
10 HC Graham, *Social Life...*, op cit
11 *Ibid*
12 *Ibid*
13 MacRobert, AE, *Transactions, op cit.*
14 Muter, Rev Robert, OSA, Stewartry of Kirkcudbright, Parish of Kirkcudbright, 1792
15 Ramage, CT, *op cit.*
16 OSA, County of Dumfriesshire, Caerlaverock Parish 1791.
17 Ramage, CT, *op cit.*
18 Train, Joseph, letter of 31 March 1829, *op cit.* The list of funeral expenses is reproduced word for word in the introduction to the subsequent 1830 edition of *Old Mortality*.
19 *Ibid*
20 Grierson, TB, manuscript notebook pp62-3, Dumfries Observatory Museum.
21 Joseph Train to Sir Walter Scott, 7th June 1829, from *Letters received by Sir Walter Scott*, labelled *Mr Train*, National Library of Scotland MS874
22 *Ibid*
23 Train, Joseph, letter to Sir Walter Scott 31 March 1829, *op cit.*
24 *Ibid*
25 *Letters of Sir Walter Scott, 18April 1829*, Vol.XI, 1828-31, ed. HJC Grierson.
26 Black, WG, *Dictionary of National Biography* 1895. The article refers to Nathaniel Paterson's *Letters to his Family*, 1874, referred to in the previous chapter.
27 John Langhorne, 'The Wallflower', from *Poetical Works*, 1766

CHAPTER TEN

THE LEGACY

The Character

The *Magnum Opus* edition of the W*averley* novels, including *The Tale of Old Mortality*, was a huge commercial success. The latter had to be reprinted within six months of its initial publication and on several more occasions, even while the rest of new series was being rolled out between 1831 and 1833. Altogether the new edition allowed Scott to repay the majority of his debts before his death. This despite the fact that the stress of its production contributed to his demise before the full series was republished. The subsequent sale of the copyright to new publishers in 1847 completely paid off the debts of his estate and the books, collectively and individually, have remained in continuous print to this day.

Interest in Scott and his work was further fuelled by a giant biography of the author produced within just a few years of his death by John Gibson Lockhart, his son-in-law, to which Joseph Train inevitably contributed. More significantly, the renewed interest also translated into a preoccupation with the characters invented by Scott for his novels or, in the case of Old Mortality, drawn from historical figures. Several of them caught the public imagination and became immensely popular.

They included Jeanie Deans, the "true-hearted, honest girl" of *Heart of Midlothian*, Dirk Hatteraick, the old smuggler in *Guy Mannering* and of course the eponymous heroes of *Rob Roy* and *Ivanhoe*, all of whom, with others, are depicted on the Scott Monument, in Edinburgh, erected to the memory of the author by public subscription in 1840. The characters drew their popularity from the very status of the novels themselves, which were romantic histories and rollicking adventure stories, but also because they were each depicted with complex individual dimensions of their own which gave those stories and adventures a more personal touch.

In the case of *Old Mortality*, the eponymous stonecutter, though not a central character of the novel, is introduced at the outset as a contemporary link to a bygone era. The Covenanting period, with its range of fanatical and mutually intolerant antagonists, was not a setting to which many of Scott's readers would have been ordinarily sympathetic: Scott referred in his novel to the "ill-appreciated motives which caused... hatred and hostility while in this valley of darkness, blood and tears."[1] But, as depicted by Scott, the character for whom Robert Paterson provided the model *could* gain popular sympathy for a number of the human traits he displayed, good and bad.

These included his obvious dedication to a cause, and his apparent hardiness in that cause – Scott referred to him more than once as a "pilgrim" - but also his famous grumpiness and even his zealous nit-picking of aspects of religious observance. In the introduction to the 1830 edition of the novel, for example, Scott recalled Paterson being in a "bad humour" when he said he met him in the churchyard at Dunnotar, with "no freedom for conversation with us. His spirit", he added in a reference to the strict Cameronian dislike for music in churches,

> "had been sorely vexed by hearing, in a certain Aberdonian kirk, the psalmody directed by a pitch-pipe, or some similar instrument, which was to Old Mortality the abomination of abominations."

And in the first chapter of the novel Scott referred to Paterson's "Motives of the most sincere, though fanciful devotion" while putting in his mouth a long diatribe against the feeble morals and lack of stamina of modern churchgoers.

Scott's readers, one feels, were being invited through the character of Old Mortality to admire the earnest devotion of a simpler age while patting themselves on the back for being part of a modern audience that could view such puritanical outpourings with a faint air of ridicule.

Monuments in Stone
In an age before mass media, the preoccupation of early Victorians with popular literary and historical characters was addressed not just through talks and lectures or illustrations in weekly or monthly periodicals but also through life size carvings of their favourites, many of which formed part of static or touring exhibitions. No self-respecting new industrial town, for example, could develop without a monument to distant heroes such as William Wallace or Robert the Bruce – or more recent heroes, such as Sir Walter Scott, as we have seen - while, in the years following the poet Robert Burns' death, several town squares, parks, gardens and other public spaces, especially in the south-west of Scotland, began to display stone carvings of characters from his works, such as Tam O'Shanter or Souter Johnnie.

In fact, Burns' characters set an early precedent for the touring exhibition when the sculptor James Thom, a native of Ayrshire, displayed his bust of the poet and carvings of his more famous characters in Edinburgh in 1828 – an event which Scott attended - and in London in 1829 prior to their being erected below Burns' Monument in his birthplace of Alloway. Thom, a self-taught sculptor who apparently carved by sight rather than to a design, later moved to the USA where he continued to earn a living through commissions of public statues, largely for a Scottish emigrant market. His statue group of *Old Mortality and his Pony*, erected in 1842, still stands in Laurel Hill cemetery in Philadelphia.

Meanwhile, towards the end of 1838 or the beginning of 1839, the sculptor John Currie (or Corrie as it is sometimes written) was commissioned by the residents of Balmaclellan village – basking in the fame occasioned by the novel - to produce a statue group of Paterson and his pony for their churchyard. As a measure of the popularity of this initiative, the cost of the commission, £150, was raised in subscriptions of 6d each.

Currie was an aspiring young artist from Lochfoot, just west of Dumfries, who went on to make a name for himself in the region and nationally through commissions of public sculptures of local worthies and the ornate decoration of building facades. In and around Dumfries, for example, he carved the facade of the former Dumfries and Galloway Royal Infirmary with various classical figures. The spiral-curved sandstone chimneys on top of several country houses in the region are also attributed to him.

The result of Currie's commission for Balmaclellan was a rather languid figure of Old Mortality, posed in an unlikely reclining position, with his mallet on the ground in front and a saddled pony standing beside him. With an eye to his career and realising the popularity of Scott's characters at the time, Currie took the opportunity afforded by this early commission to make several copies of the group, as a model for which he is reported[2] to have used an eighty year-old local resident of Balmaclellan (this could have been Robert junior who was still alive, aged eighty-two). Through the family, who were still resident in the village, he was also able to borrow Paterson senior's own tools from Joseph Train.

Once completed, the original statuary group went on tour, starting in Edinburgh in March 1839 and going on to be exhibited in a number of northern English cities. The *Liverpool Mercury* for 14th June 1839, for example, advertised:

> "Old Mortality & his Pony. Now exhibiting in Bold Street, opposite Concert Street, Currie's celebrated group of Sir Walter Scott's 'Old Mortality' & his Pony, sculptured in stone, the size of life. Open from 10 in the morning till dusk. Admission one shilling. A History of Old Mortality with some account of the artist may be had at the Exhibition, price sixpence each."

However, when they were eventually returned to the village, the statues were found to have suffered from wear and tear and possibly a little vandalism by visitors seeking physical mementos. According to newspaper reports[3], the ears were missing off the donkey and the head of Old Mortality was damaged. (Judging by the evidence of the remaining statues, the mallet was lost along the way as well.) The group was consequently placed in the grounds of Holm Farm, once tenanted by Walter Paterson, less than half a mile from the centre of the village, where they remained, weatherbeaten and neglected, but acquiring recognition as a listed monument in 1970. In 2000, as part of Millennium celebrations, the local community council obtained the funds necessary to restore and re-locate the group to Balmaclellan churchyard.

Another copy of the group was shortly afterwards raffled by Currie, at 10/- a ticket. *The Dumfries Times*[4] contained an advert for the lottery which was held on 25 October 1840, prior to which the group was exhibited at the Assembly Hall in the town itself. The winning ticket belonged to a Dr John Sinclair, a young naval surgeon who was stationed in Portsmouth at the time, preparing to sail for Africa in the schooner *Excellent*. On 26 October, the night before sailing, he and several friends hired gigs and set out for Southampton on a last bout of shore leave but were unfortunately involved in a collision with a wagon near Titchfield.[5]

Sinclair died from his wounds, unaware that he had the winning ticket for the Old Mortality statue group in his pocket, something that was only discovered when his possessions were returned to Dumfries. However, the group was later presented to Dumfries Observatory Museum, apparently in accordance with Sinclair's wishes, by his family. The Museum had only recently been founded (in 1835) and the statues were donated with a plaque in Sinclair's memory. And there they still stand, protected by a glass cupola, with a magnificent view west over to the Galloway Hills.

Another copy, of a reclining figure of Old Mortality only, plus the statue of a Cameronian peasant, were found in storage in the village of Moniaive in 1988 by Currie's great nephew. These stood for a while in Balmaclellan but were eventually donated to Newton Stewart Museum where they now stand in the grounds.[6] Thus the remaining sculptures of Paterson are well spread across the region which he travelled so extensively while a final statue, also by Currie but this time of the standing figure of Old Mortality, is included amongst the sculptures fixed to the Scott Memorial in Edinburgh.

The Historians' Views
Having been unearthed and preserved for posterity by Train, no matter how imperfectly, the story of Paterson *the individual* was revisited by a succession of Victorian 'antiquarians' or historians through the nineteenth and early twentieth centuries. Though none of them fully addressed the assumptions underlying the popular account contained in Scott's novel, or checked their facts in some cases, each added a little more background to his life and judged his motives from their own particular angle, so advancing the story and keeping Old Mortality in the public view.

Thomas Boyle Grierson (1818-89) of Thornhill was, as we saw in the last chapter, a collector of artefacts and curiosities who, true to form, unearthed a witness to Paterson's funeral expenses which he then transcribed in his notebook. The notes are useful for corroborating elements of the story and location of Paterson's death and therefore adding to the debate over Train's version of events but say little else about the man.

Crawford Tait Ramage (1803-78) was a writer on an eclectic range of subjects who was a student of, and later taught at, Wallace Hall Academy in Closeburn, Nithsdale. His main contribution to our story was through his 1876 work *Drumlanrig Castle and the Douglases* (including the *Early History and Ancient Remains of Durisdeer, Closeburn, and Morton*) in which, as we have seen in several previous chapters, he reproduced the original text of Robert junior's letter of September 1827 to Joseph Train.

Ramage's source for the document, and for a version of the story of John Paterson, appears to have been the then minister of Balmaclellan, the Reverend George Murray. Born in New Galloway, Murray was minister at Balmaclellan from 1838-43 and again from 1851-81 and was described as a "zealous antiquary".[7] He was the author of the parish entry in the New Statistical Account of 1845 where it is clear from the sources which he cites for his description of local antiquities that he was a friend of Joseph Train – which rather pleasingly closes the circle.

Based on his access to the original letter, Ramage cast doubt on the popular view that Paterson's lifestyle derived from his Covenanting beliefs but he was still unquestioning in his use of anecdotes provided by Train which supported the same narrative. Ramage, it seemed, liked a good story and nowhere was this more evident than in his belief in the 'Napoleon' connection relating to John Paterson, as described in Chapter Eight. According to Alexander Anderson in his memoir of the Reverend Nathaniel Paterson[8], Old Mortality's grandson, Ramage wrote to Elizabeth Bonaparte (née Patterson) at her home in Paris in 1870 to enquire of the connection. The curt denial of the story which Ramage received apparently did not satisfy his image of events and he chose to ignore it until Nathaniel Paterson junior (Old Mortality's great-grandson) established the facts while on a visit to Baltimore in 1873.

James King Hewison (1853-1941) probably wrote the most extensively on Paterson, particularly in his series of monthly newspaper articles during 1898, which were eventually collected together as *Chiselprints of Old Mortality*, but also in passing in his histories of Dumfriesshire (1912)[9] and the Church of Scotland (1913)[10], respectively. He was born and died in Thornhill, in Nithsdale, and in between was a church minister in Stair, in the west of the region, and then for the Isle of Bute, but maintained a specific interest and expertise in the Covenanters throughout his life.

This was the prism through which Hewison viewed Paterson's exertions. Although he was an astute researcher who corrected several of the 'facts' in Train's account and to whom we are indebted for his record of the churchyards and even specific headstones which Paterson may have carved or repaired, he never doubted that his subject's motives were anything other than devotion to the Covenanting tradition.

William Shillinglaw Crockett (1866-1945) was the minister of Tweedsmuir parish, in the Scottish Borders between Moffat and Peebles and a prolific writer on all things relating to Scott, his novels and his home at Abbotsford. He also wrote a number of popular books on the characters in Scott's novels, describing their historical background but also relating them to places in the Borders and Dumfriesshire for the benefit of Edwardian tourists.

In his *The Scott Originals: Characters in the Waverley novels* (1912) he included a chapter on Old Mortality which largely sets out the established story – based, it would appear, on Robert junior's letter - but which also contained some new facts about Paterson's birth and early life. Similar to Ramage, Crockett noted that the original source for the story said nothing of Paterson's Covenanting beliefs and placed more emphasis on his profit-making motive of producing headstones for carriage into Galloway and Kirkcudbrightshire. The impetus for Paterson's decision, Crockett said, was that he sought to exploit the trend towards marking burials with decorated, commemorative stones.

Seeking to balance his assessment, however, Crockett added that Paterson's decision coincided with a strong desire among members of the Covenanting population of the west and upland parts of the region to have the last resting place of their martyrs commemorated in similar fashion. By choosing to follow one path, he implied, Paterson – inevitably for that part of the country – became associated with the other.

Conclusions

Scott's encounter with Old Mortality in Dunnotar churchyard all those years previously, if it happened at all, was no more than a brief one he admitted when he presented Paterson's life story in the introduction to the 1830 edition. The long evening of conversation with the old man which he originally described in Chapter One of the novel was therefore a fiction, intended both to establish a living connection with the 'Killing Times' and to create an atmosphere.

The 'meeting' may, in fact, only have been a fleeting glimpse of, or passing exchange with, a local stonemason plying his trade in the churchyard, whose costume and bearing in the twilight of a summer's evening were brought to mind by his conversation with Joseph Train when the idea for the novel was taking shape in 1816. Scott, after all, did not know much about Paterson at the time of writing, despite supposedly interrogating the old man for his life story, so it seems unlikely that he knew who he had encountered that evening. Or it may have been entirely the product of his very fertile imagination, spurred on perhaps by the barest details furnished by his future researcher-in-chief at the beginning of their relationship. Train himself said that he did not get to meet Paterson's son, the source for the more detailed information that he eventually forwarded to Scott, until 1827.

In between the two editions of the novel, Scott had actually become acquainted with Paterson's grandson, Nathaniel, but, if they held conversations of any length at all over dinner at Abbotsford, it doesn't seem to have provided the novelist with any more detailed background until Train's fortuitous letter as the proofs for the revised edition were being assembled in 1829. Whatever the foundations for Scott's chance encounter, we can be sure that he invented the character that was to become Old Mortality, and possibly even his nickname, even if he had some sound research on which to base it.

Despite all of that, distinguishing between the character of Old Mortality and the real life individual that was Robert Paterson can be difficult. The impression of both that has survived over the two centuries since *The Tale of Old Mortality* was first published is shaped, on the one hand, by the literary creation that Scott used to introduce the theme and mood of the rest of his novel and, on the other, by the biographical outline provided by Train which seems to have been designed to fit the original mould.

Scott's depiction of the fictional stonecutter is remarkably similar to the little that we know of Paterson himself in his old age. The clothes that Mortality wore in the novel were not unlike later descriptions of Paterson's appearance given by Hewison's combined sources and Ramage's witness, Mrs McLellan, though they were not untypical of the appearance of the rural peasantry generally of the early eighteenth century, which Scott could have elicited from other sources.

There was also the famous sourness with which Scott coloured his character, a trait which Mrs McLellan reported as well. Describing Robert junior, the shoemaker who lived in her village, she said he was "badtempered, but very honest and truthful", adding that the whole family had "dure tempers". This trait was, however, common to several of the Covenanters who featured in the rest of the novel and in fact Scott's stereotyping of the "western zealots" in this way was an aspect of the book that drew most criticism from contemporaries.

Scott also played on the image of Old Mortality as a throwback to a simpler, pre-industrial past – a craftsman in a machine age - in which principles and values meant more than money and the luxuries it could buy. Painted with the gloss of his Covenanting zeal, this is not dissimilar to the impression given by Train in his notes to Scott or to the view which modern readers might form themselves from the background given in the preceding chapters. They are all romantic notions of both the character and the man created by Scott with Train's help.

Set against the popular image, however, is the evidence collected in this book which suggests that there were crucial differences between the semi-fictional character and the real life individual. Key amongst these are the motives for Paterson's itinerant lifestyle.

The view of Robert junior, the little that we know of the old man's pattern of income and expenditure and the way in which he appears to have fitted into a tradition of commercial travellers in the eighteenth century all suggest that it *is* valid to argue for Paterson severing his domestic ties as much for financial motives as religious ones. It would also seem from his son's letter, the decisions made in relation to his personal life and early career and the mix of stonecutting – including the mix of headstones - on which he worked until his middle years, that Paterson's attraction to the Covenanting cause grew on him as he mingled more and more with people from that tradition, rather than being an outlook with which he was naturally imbued.

Within this more prosaic view of his motives, it is also possible to discern a quite pragmatic aspect to Paterson's activities. These include the logical way in which he sought out and moved between sources for the stone he needed for his trade, the recruitment of his son as an apprentice, the apparent development over the years of a base within the west of the region – with a range of contacts on whom he could rely for favours – the use of waterborne transport for the carriage of stone where appropriate or the resilience which he displayed into his old age for travelling about a quite remote and hilly region with other blocks of stone in tow, hiring a pony where necessary or, eventually, coming to rely on the animal for transport. This pattern of practical activity conflicts with the popular view of the old man as an ethereal sort, driven by a simple religious zeal to wander between the homes of like-minded souls.

On the other hand, it is probably wrong to go further than this and to argue that the traditional link between Paterson and the Covenanting cause was simply one of association: that is to say, between the increasingly popular fashion for decorated headstones which he exploited, and the parallel rise in demand for Covenanting memorials which he had inevitably to accommodate as part of his work. As Hewison said, it is possible to see how Paterson's "sepulchral occupation... invested him with an air of reverence"[11] which may have created a false impression in contemporaries – and in later commentators - of what drove him.

Although this is a tempting analysis it is contradicted by the fact that Paterson chose to move away from Morton parish to concentrate on Kirkcudbrightshire, Galloway and Ayrshire. His later decision to move his family to Balmaclellan, in the heartland of the Covenanting tradition, further negates this view. The fashion for headstones was a national one, after all, not confined to the more ardent

Presbyterians in the deep south-west of the region, and yet Paterson – as we have seen – went in that direction.

Talking of geography, and given the want of proof to the contrary, the documentary evidence and various testaments unearthed in this book suggest that Paterson's 'wanderings' were also more limited than tradition would have it. Robert junior's letter, the various documents and sightings which place him around Kircudbright, and even Joseph Train's despatches to Scott all confirm the route traced by Hewison from the evidence of the stones on which Paterson appears to have worked. Scott said that Old Mortality was known in "various parts of Scotland" and, as discussed, claims to have encountered him in the north-east of the country. Train, meanwhile, could see his work "spread over nearly all of the Lowlands". However, the evidence suggests that Paterson restricted his activity very largely to the counties already listed, albeit that he appears to have regularly criss-crossed that region.

Paterson, we can conclude, was not one of those for whom "Presbyterian principle has become an inheritance and a 'dour' sense of freedom, an instinct by heredity"[12], as Hewison described his fellow residents in Morton and Balmaclellan. There was a logic and a pattern to his career, and to his life, dictated as much by the materials of his chosen trade as to the fashions of the period and the conditions of the region in which he lived. Paterson, in one sense, fitted into his life and times.

The fact that he chose to pursue that lifestyle into what was, for his contemporaries, extreme old age, despite the option to retire comfortably, marked him out in the fast moving social and economic circumstances of the century as an eccentric at worst. As Scott wrote to Train in relation to the story of Paterson's life with which he had furnished him, "A strain of genius (too highly toned in the old patriarch) seems to have run through the whole family."[13]

To his contemporaries and near-contemporaries, who viewed the progress of their society as an entirely good thing, Paterson – or at least the character of the old man that he represented - was perhaps someone to be patronised or viewed as an object of ridicule. The Victorians were more sympathetic. They saw in him someone who represented the successful struggle for freedom of worship and perhaps as a man who led an enviable, if unconventional, form of independence at a time when an increasing number of people were being tied down to a salaried existence.

Today, in a less spiritual, more material but also more politically-correct society, our view of Paterson is necessarily more complicated. People probably think it less important to dissect his religious beliefs but struggle with how someone could feel sufficiently motivated to adopt the lifestyle he did. They can admire his apparently simple existence but would consider his asceticism distinctly odd. They can sympathise with the community values of those whose company he sought out, though noting that he shunned that very type of existence through his nomadic lifestyle, while his apparent neglect of his family would only meet with criticism. Ultimately, we have to respect Paterson's sense of purpose and determination, as a survivor in an era of change, while keeping that awkward distance which is reserved for those who choose to follow the life of an outsider.

Notes

1 Scott, Sir Walter, chapter 1 of *Old Mortality,* Penguin 1985
2 *Dumfries & Galloway Notes and Queries,* ed. C Mackie, 1913. There are several entries relating to newspaper reports and correspondence from the period.
3 Dumfries Library Monuments Index – the reports cited were from *The Dumfries Courier and Herald* in 1840.
4 *Dumfries Times,* 6 October 1840
5 Dumfries & Galloway Courier, 18 November 1840
6 Dumfries Library Monuments Index, *op cit*
7 *Fastii Ecclesiasticus Scotticanae,* ed. Hew Scott DD, Oliver & Boyd, 1917.
8 Anderson, Alexander, preface and memoir in *Letters To His Family,* Nathaniel Paterson 1874
9 Hewison, JK, A History of Dumfriesshire, 1912
10 Hewison, JK, *The Covenanters: A History of the Church in Scotland from the Reformation to the Revolution,* 1913
11 Hewison, JK, *Chiselprints of Old Mortality, op cit*
12 *ibid*
13 *Letters of Sir Walter Scott, 18 April 1829,* Vol.XI, 1828-31, ed. HJC Grierson

ACKNOWLEDGEMENTS

The support and assistance of staff in the Ewart Library, Dumfries, Dumfries Museum and Hawick Library in the research for this book is gratefully acknowledged.

Thanks also to Flora Burns for sense-checking and Jill Ringland for proof-reading the manuscript.

All images reproduced in this book are from the collection of the author with the exception of the carved image of Joseph Train which is taken from the Future Museum website and reproduced with the permission of Dumfries Museum.

The image of Sir Walter Scott's bust by Sir Francis Chantrey was taken in Abbotsford House.

The image of Closeburn Castle was taken with the assistance of the Kirkpatrick family.

The images of the original Caldons Wood gravestone and the Old Mortality statue at Newton Stewart Museum are reproduced with the permission of the trustees of the museum.

The image of Old Mortality's leather notebook was taken with the assistance of staff at Dumfries Museum and reproduced with their permission.

The supply of and permission to reproduce the following documents is also acknowledged:
- Engraving of 'Old Mortality' from *Scott's Worthies,* WS Crockett, and image of Exterior of Haggisha' in c.1908, both by Hawick Museum and Library Service.
- The list of Paterson's funeral expenses as transcribed by Thomas Boyle, by Dumfries Museum.

telling us they cannot. There is no easy way to do these things. Hurt, pain, grief and anger come with this territory because we are talking about real endings. It is a sort of death, and things – particularly relationships – are not going to be the same again."

Typically, David Stevens reminded the Community that even the meaning of "Corrymeela" in the Gaelic had been revised from "the hill of harmony" to "the lumpy crossing-place". He said, "That more truly expresses the reality. We have to deal with the reality of imperfection, and recognise that things are often simply lumpy. And Corrymeela is still a crossing-place, and there are few of them in Northern Ireland."

Equally realistically, he forecast a period of uncertainty in the political life of Northern Ireland. He said, "We need to understand what the restoration of devolution means and will do. It is another step in a long journey. It is not the end of the journey. At best it may be a sort of half-resolution, and there are huge uncertainties hanging over it. How it will work – if it works at all – will be through trade-offs and clientalism, and it will not be a pretty sight."

As well as the realism in Stevens' message, there was also a renewed challenge, and a sense of hope. He said, "There is still a need to look beyond tiredness, self-absorption and money pressures to what we are called to be and do in new times. This is a long-term business and we need to think how we can inspire the new generation – the people who are really going to carry us into a promised land."

He also referred to James Alison, the Catholic theologian, who claimed that there can be "an apparent heaviness in reconciliation work. But he goes on to say that from a Christian perspective this is profoundly wrong, that we should start from 'the extraordinary sensation of being in luck, of having fallen, despite ourselves on our feet, in the midst of ridiculously good fortune'." Stevens also asks, "Is not that our actual situation is Corrymeela? Have we not, despite ourselves, despite all the nonsense we find ourselves in at times, fallen on our feet in the midst of ridiculously good fortune?"

Perhaps another way of putting it, with Biblical undertones, would be to observe that for the true Corrymeela the "yoke is heavy but the burden is light". The future for the Community will depend not only on outside and internal factors but also on the spirituality, strength and vision of the members themselves. It will also depend on Corrymeela's ability to remain endlessly flexible, as its founder Ray Davey has advised, and to know what lies in its own heart – even to the point of disbandment or a total re-grouping, if that ever seems necessary.

After more than forty years of existence, what has Corrymeela really achieved? Duncan Morrow, who has spent so much of his life within, and contributing to, Corrymeela says that he is unnerved by the word 'achievement', which speaks to him of actions, set goals and effectiveness, or of deliberate actions for specific purposes.

He says, "I am very clear that if Corrymeela had defined its purposes in terms of 'key performance indicators' or 'targets' then they would have been a catastrophic distraction in 1969 or 1985. However, the challenge for a Christian Community is not to deliver targets, but must be to bear witness to the reality of love in the world, whatever the circumstances, and through staying close to this faith, to transform the world for all those who then come into contact with that reality. And the test of 'achievement' is how well, through testing circumstances, did we keep the faith?"

For Morrow the knowledge that "there is a love for each and all of us, which survives longer than every challenge, including death, makes all the difference. When this was real to me, I found myself living with other people who were officially my enemy, but who were now my friends, bringing new dimensions of insight and experience to my own life."

Corrymeela has been 'a big part' of his experience of what this theology might mean. Morrow says that "In its best moments, Corrymeela is a community of people who are 'on to something', something utterly important and hardly open to description – but it matters. Of course most of the time we found ourselves failing, and we are forced to learn each time how utterly dependent we are on forgiving and being forgiven to have a future at all. What we did, especially what Corrymeela is known for, by being a place of openness and acceptance in a Northern Ireland consumed by fear and hatred, depended – and still depends utterly – upon being open to what was given to us, what came to hand."

He believes that it was not up to the Community to evaluate "the practical contribution that witnessing to love makes, but I am sure that it remains and acts in very strange ways. Most importantly, in the Northern Ireland context, it was part of the evidence that hatred and fear did not define, or contain, all of reality. And that mattered at a very difficult time, in very complicated ways."

What made the witness of Corrymeela possible in the 1970s and 80s "was ultimately not the Community's ecumenical nature, its 'Hill of Harmony' image or its willingness to talk to all when other avenues seemed closed; but through all of those activities, in sustaining a practical and slightly credible witness to the God of all the victims, who loves all of His children, and grieves for every lost sheep in the midst of a veritable whirlwind of bitterness, violence and hatred."

In the Northern Ireland of the Troubles, this translated into a task of welcome, of human meeting and contact, of worship and of eating together and of mutual service, but not primarily one of "speaking at" or "preaching to" people. Duncan Morrow says that Corrymeela's inevitable calling was to be a contrast to the culture in which it lived, but not as another "angry culture" to the "surrounding culture".

He says, "No matter how much killing there was, it was made up of our brothers and sisters in whom we also repeatedly recognised ourselves. We couldn't condemn or 'win over' this world, but we could try to point to a way out, on the basis that we already knew that it was our redemption too."

So what was the achievement? Morrow says, "The achievement, if there was one, was to give credible and practical meaning to reconciliation in a world which had lost any sense of it, except through victory over others. And much of that vision was carried out by people and groups and organisations who were not directly Corrymeela, but were either directly or indirectly made safe or given confidence by what Corrymeela was grappling to do."

However, Corrymeela had failures, and these were in many ways the underside of its achievements. Morrow says, "So often we were hypocritical, doing to members and in our pompous judgement of others, exactly the same things as we condemned others for doing. There are too many stories of personal injury, which belie our self-congratulation as a Christian community, to be comfortable about. There is truth, too, in the accusation that Corrymeela in Ballycastle was an unreal fairyland, too disconnected from the real challenges of inter-community violence to make a lasting difference. There is also more than a grain of truth in the accusation that many issues were ignored, or not given due weight."

Duncan Morrow believes, like others inside and outside the Community, that Corrymeela was far from perfect. He says, "That imperfection was the vital grit in the oyster which taught us the paradoxical truth, that without forgiveness and mercy we are all lost. This was a Community who were on to something more important for human life than killing for national sovereignty or religious purity, and that *was* and *is* important."

Corrymeela was a candle in the darkness, when it was especially dark in Northern Ireland. Morrow recalls that "The task was to bring reconciliation to life in a world which did not believe in it, and was not sure whether it wished it. Sustaining a commitment to reconciliation while a civil war rages may be extremely difficult, but it does not create a clear boundary and clarity of purpose and mission."

There are paradoxes. "At a time when reconciliation has become a 'buzz word' of a whole political class, and central to a wider British and Irish concern to bury the enmities of Northern Ireland in common pursuit of success in the modern economy, the particularity of an ecumenical Christian Community is less. The result may well be that Corrymeela has to become less visible, less famous. It may even be that the Community which was Corrymeela eventually disappears."

However, Duncan Morrow, like others, believes that this need not be so. He says, "The task of Christian communities is endless, to witness for real reconciliation, to demonstrate real openness to all, and to search for the practical meaning of inclusion in the modern world. Corrymeela was never a meeting place for Catholics and Protestants as representatives of institutions, but as a place where Catholics and Protestants met, and found each other's humanity, and learned something important about what it meant to have life together."

In all of this, the story of the past is a strength and not a weakness, "but only if it is a model of the spirit with which we engage in the issues of this age, rather than a practice which has to be carbon-copied, even though the challenges have changed. Yet a contrast to the exclusions which the world puts up is as needed as ever."

Reconciliation, Morrow believes, is not an "event". He says, "In Northern Ireland, the legacy of the past is huge, and it will continue. Trust will never be learned by inciting people to trust one another, but only by making it possible through generosity and openness to meet and learn. As Northern Ireland changes, so the people who live here will change, and the challenges of meeting and learning will become more, rather than less, complicated."

Duncan Morrow believes that Corrymeela can find an ongoing role in it all. He says, "Finding justice without revenge, making peace with real enemies, meeting people after deep injury, seeking to make faith meaningful and real – these are all tasks requiring urgent attention. They just have a different colour and order now. Corrymeela's experience of practical engagement with the unknown in faith is as central as ever. And if it is not Corrymeela, it will have to be reinvented."

EPILOGUE

THE POLITICIANS IN NORTHERN IRELAND, and its people, have travelled a long way in recent months. The elections in early 2007 gave the politicians a mandate to get on with the business of governing. Despite all the odds, they duly obliged by forging an unlikely agreement, and by starting to tackle the issues, such as housing, education and the economy, which people on all sides had wished for a long time to be addressed by local representatives.

The words of the political leaders, some of whom were previously not talking to one another, underlined the long road that had been travelled, but with commendable speed, towards the end. Dr Ian Paisley said, "Today, at long last, we are starting upon the road – I emphasise *starting* – which I believe will take us to lasting peace in our Province... Northern Ireland has come to a time of peace, a time when hate will no longer rule."

Martin McGuinness said, "We know that this will not be easy, and the road we are embarking on will have many twists and turns. Ian Paisley, I want to wish you all the best as we step forward towards the greatest, yet most exciting, challenges of our lives." It was, indeed, a day which no one thought would ever arrive.

Corrymeela has travelled a long way since 1965, but it has kept at its heart the core values of its early vision which has sustained the Community through so much change and turmoil. That vision, shared with others, has been best expressed in the life and leadership of Ray Davey himself, whose moving and life-changing experience of the destruction of Dresden, and its renewal, is so symbolic of a powerfully inspiring message in the Book of Revelation, "Behold, I make all things new."

Today the city of Dresden, only a short rail journey from Berlin, has emerged from a long historical winter, symbolised by the magnificent Frauenkirche, which has been rebuilt to its former glory after its almost total destruction by the Allied bombing during the Second World War. In that city also stands the historic Kreuzkirche with its Cross of Nails, where Ray Davey brought his message of hope and reconciliation, some forty years after the destruction of Dresden.

It is appropriate, therefore, that the first and last words of the Corrymeela story to date, belong to Ray Davey himself. In his *War Diaries* he describes how, as a prisoner just outside Dresden, he visited the devastated city after the Allied bombing. In an entry dated 20 March 1945 he wrote: "Today, I went down to Dresden and saw it all for myself. All the buildings I had come to know so well – the Zwinger, the Hofkirche, the Frauenkirche, the Neus Rathaus, the Semperoper, the Schloss, etc, are now at best shells and mostly rubble. Postplatz is unrecognisable, the Zwinger is burnt out and looks like an ancient monument just unearthed. In the streets there is an unusual silence, few people about; scattered groups of British or Russian POWs leisurely working on the ruins. I felt strangely uncomfortable walking around the sorrows of this once beautiful city."

Some forty years later, Ray Davey returned to Dresden as part of a group from the British Churches Council, and he spoke at a service in the Kreuzkirche. He recalls, "I spoke very simply and directly as to how I felt about being back, how the last time I had been a prisoner and indeed an enemy in their city. I described something of the pain and hurt we prisoners had felt at the loss of many of our comrades who had died because of forced marches from the east, and others who had been cruelly treated

"Then I went on to describe how I and my fellow prisoners had felt about the terrible air-raids, and all the death and suffering that followed. But now today we were meeting at the one table and sharing the one Bread, and were mutually forgiven and reconciled by the one Lord. I felt very much that I was not only speaking for myself, but for all my fellow prisoners who had been with me away back forty years ago.

"But it wasn't only for them, but also for all those in our own country who today pray and yearn for peace and healing among nations. I believe that we in that service together were being visible signs of that peace and reconciliation and oneness that God wills."

The service led to a remarkable coincidence. That night Ray and Kathleen went to the famous Semperoper (Opera House) that had been so badly damaged in the air-raids and had just re-opened on 13 February 1985 – the fortieth anniversary of its destruction. On that terrible night in 1945, Carl von Weber's opera *Der Freischutz* was being performed, as it was during the re-opening night. Ray recalls that, during the interval, a lady sitting next to Kathleen started talking to her. She and her husband had been to that day's service in the Kreuzkirche, and she had recognised the Daveys.

Ray recalls, "She went on to explain just how much it had meant to her husband and herself. They had come over from Munich in West Germany, and had decided to go to the Kreuzkirche because her husband had been confirmed there. At the time of the air-raids, her husband, although he was only sixteen, was in the army and staying in barracks."

During the air raids, his mother, his six-year-old brother and both grandparents were killed. "Ever since, he had been filled with hatred and bitterness against the British and Americans, and simply could not forgive. But being present at that service and seeing what happened, he felt something speak to him and he broke down in tears and realised that now he could forgive."

Back in 1945, shortly after the Dresden bombing and as the war drew to a close with the defeat of Germany, Ray Davey reflected in his *War Diaries* about the meaning of Easter. He was joyful, and yet he remembered the ashes of Dresden; so many people had died, including his former comrades. He felt like leaving Easter to "the ancient Festival of Spring" but he concluded, "Somehow I can't do that. For me, it means that I want God and when I interpret Easter in terms of God, then I get peace."

Easter, he reflected, was not an escape from the mystery of evil and pain. "It's God's answer to it. It's not an attempt to take us from the grimness of our 20th century world, but a call to face it and see through it and see God. Like our world, the drama moves down into the valley of death and destruction, but it climbs up the other side into life and victory over death. Here God sets His stamp on the real inward qualities of life's character of love, joy and courage, and shows us that these are the final things of life."

And that is all that needs to be said.

NOTES

CHAPTER ONE
1 From Little Gidding.
2 In an interview with Judith Cole in the *Belfast Telegraph*, October 3, 2005.
3 *The War Diaries*, published by The Brehon Press, Belfast, 2005.
4 Ibid Page 101.
5 Ibid Page 147.
6 Ibid Page 198.
7 Foreword to Ray Davey's book *Take Away This Hate*, published by The Corrymeela Press.
8 In an interview with Alf McCreary for *Corrymeela Connections* Volume 5 No 2.
9 *Journey of Hope – Sources of the Corrymeela Vision* by John Morrow, published by The Corrymeela Press, Page 14.
10 In an interview with the author.
11 *The Corrymeela Story*, page 11, published by the Community.
12 Ibid.

CHAPTER TWO
1 Corrymeela pamphlet, page 4.
2 Dr David Stevens, Leader's Address, November 2004.

CHAPTER THREE
1 Leader's Report 1965-78.
2 Corrymeela Introductory Paper.
3 *A History of Ulster*, published by the Blackstaff Press, pp 622-623.
4 In an interview with the author.
5 In an interview with the author.
6 In a conversation with the author.

7 *Lost Lives* by David McKittrick, Seamus Kelters, Brian Feeney, and Chris Thornton, published by Mainstream Publishing, page 61.
8 Recollections of Alf McCreary, who was then a senior writer on the staff of the *Belfast Telegraph*.
9 Corrymeela Leader's Report, November 1979.
10 Ibid.

CHAPTER FOUR
1 Quoted in *Corrymeela – The Search for Peace* by Alf McCreary, published by Christian Journals Ltd, 1975, page 18.
2 Ibid.
3 Ibid.
4 In an interview with the author.

CHAPTER FIVE
1 Quoted from *Tried By Fire* by Alf McCreary, page 87, published by Marshall Pickering, London, 1986, and earlier by Christian Journals Ltd, Belfast.
2 Ibid pp 89-91
3 Ibid page 92.
4 Ibid page 94.
5 *A Channel of Peace* by Ray Davey, pp 18-19, published by Marshall Pickering, 1993.
6 *Profiles of Hope* by Alf McCreary, pp 43-52, published by Christian Journals, 1981.
7 Ibid.
8 Ibid.
9 *Take Away This Hate* by Ray Davey, published by Corrymeela.

CHAPTER SIX
1 *Corrymeela – The Search for Peace*, pp 30-31.
2 In background notes prepared at the request of the author.
3 In a lengthy background note, prepared at the request of the author.

CHAPTER SEVEN
1 These figures used to be easily obtainable from the security forces, but this has been less so in the recent years of relative peace. The figures quoted were contained in the appendices of one of the most valuable reference works covering that period, *Northern Ireland – A Political Directory 1968-89*, complied by Dr Sydney Elliott and WD Flackes, with John Coulter, and published by the Blackstaff Press.
2 In conversation with the author on 21 July, 2006.
3 Ibid.
4 *Take Away This Hate*, published by The Corrymeela Press, pp 108-9.
5 Ibid.
6 Ibid.
7 In conversation with the author on 21 July, 2006.
9 Ibid.
10 *Corrymeela Connections* Vol 5, No 2, page 5.

CHAPTER EIGHT
1 *Journey of Hope – Sources of the Corrymeela Vision*, published by the Corrymeela Press, 1995, page 14.
2 Ibid.
3 Ibid.
4 Ibid.
5 In an interview with the author in late 2005.
6 Ibid.
7 Ibid.
8 Ibid.

9 *Journey of Hope*, page 51.
10 Ibid.
11 In an interview with the author.
12 Ibid.
15 Ibid.

CHAPTER NINE
1 In an interview with the author in early 2006.
2 Ibid.
3 Ibid.
4 Ibid.
5 The work of Summerfest will be covered in a later Chapter.
6 Evangelical Contribution on Northern Ireland.

CHAPTER TEN
1 *Northern Ireland – A Political Directory*, pp 681-89
2 *On The Road of Reconciliation*, published in 2003 by the Columba Press, pp 58-9.
3 Op. Cit. page 58.
4 The important work of Edmund and Maura Kiely has been mentioned earlier.
5 In an interview with the author.
6 Op. Cit. page 59.

CHAPTER ELEVEN
1 In an interview with the author.
2 *On the Road to Reconciliation*, page 77.

CHAPTER TWELVE
1 In an extended interview with the author in 2006.
2 *Northern Ireland – A Political Directory 1968-99*, pp56-64.
3 *Nobody's Fool* by Alf McCreary, published by Hodder and Stoughton, London, 2004, page 176.
4 This issue is also discussed in *The Land of Unlikeness – Explorations in Reconciliation* by Dr David Stevens, published by the Columba Press, 2004

5   Some of these matters will be
    discussed in a later chapter.

CHAPTER THIRTEEN
1   As described by the Reverend
    Doug Baker in a paper on
    Summerfest, prepared at the
    request of the author.
2   Ibid.
3   *On the Road To Reconciliation*, pp
    60-61.
4   Op. Cit. pp 54-55.
5   *The Land of Unlikeness*, page 11.
6   *On The Road To Reconciliation*, pp
    56-57.
7   *The Land of Unlikeness*, page 11.
8   *On the Road To Reconciliation*, page
    56.
9   In an interview with the author.

CHAPTER FOURTEEN
1   Quoted from *An Unfinished
    Journey* by Ray Davey, published by
    The Corrymeela Press.
2   Op.Cit.
3   Ibid.
4   In a conversation with the author
    in Reading.
5   In an interview with the author in
    Reading.

CHAPTER FIFTEEN
1   The author is indebted to the
    editors of the Corrymeela worship
    book, *Celebrating Together*, for
    information about The Croi and its
    contents.
2   In a paper prepared for the author.
3   In an article in *Corrymeela
    Connections*, Vol 5, No2, pp 23-24.
4   The background was explained by
    Norman Richardson in an article
    for *Corrymeela Connections* in
    January 2006.
5   *Corrymeela Connections* op.cit.
6   In notes prepared for the author.

CHAPTER SEVENTEEN
1   Published by The Columba Press
    pp 7-8.
2   Ibid.
3   Ibid.
4   Ibid.
5   The Dutch were later to make an
    important   contribution   to
    Corrymeela, as has been noted
    elsewhere.
6   Published by The Columba Press
    in 2001.
7   Op.Cit Page 19.
8   Ronnie Millar's contribution to
    Corrymeela is outlined in a later
    chapter.
9   Unless stated otherwise, David
    Stevens' remarks in this chapter
    were during a recorded interview
    with the author.

CHAPTER TWENTY
1   The conversation took place with
    this writer just before a Press
    Conference in Belfast on the day
    after the Dalai Lama visited
    Corrymeela.
2   In an interview with the author.
3   During an interview with the
    author in St Ethelburga's in August,
    2006
4   In an interview with the author in
    Belfast in December 2006.

CHAPTER TWENTY-ONE
1   In an interview with Dr David
    Stevens, the Leader of Corrymeela,
    which was published by the
    Corrymeela Magazine P l6, No 1,
    December 2005.
2   In an interview with the author in
    mid-summer 2006.
3   In an interview with the author in
    2006.
4   *The Land of Unlikeness*, published
    by The Columba Press pp 72-73.
5   In an interview with the author.
6   First published in 2001 by The
    Columba Press, page 346.